PILGRIM OF
THE CLOUDS

Poems and Essays by

Yüan Hung-tao

and

HIS BROTHERS

Translated and Introduced by

Jonathan Chaves

White Pine Press • Buffalo, New York

This book was originally published by John Weatherhill, Inc.

Some of the poems in this collection have appeared previously in the
following magazines: *Montemora, The Virginia Quarterly Review,* and *First Issue.*

Publication of this book was made possible, in part, with public funds
from the New York State Council on the Arts, a State Agency.

Printed and bound in the United States of America.

First Edition

Companions for the Journey, Volume 9

Library of Congress Control Number: 2005929024

Pubished by
White Pine Press
P.O. Box 236
Buffalo, New York 14201
www.whitepine.org

PILGRIM OF THE CLOUDS

FOR ANNA, MY WIFE

"As Long as the Sky..."

Contents

PREFACE

As with my translations of the poetry of Yang Wan-li in *Heaven My Blanket, Earth My Pillow,* I have translated the poetry and prose of the Yüan brothers into colloquial American English. Although rhyme is an element in the original poems, I have not attempted to employ it in the translations, since rhymes are much more abundant in the Chinese language than they are in English; any attempt to apply rhyme in the translations would have seemed forced and unnatural.

The writings collected in this book are not presented chronologically, but rather in a sequence suggested by mood or theme. In the cases of the poems "In Ch'ang-an There Is a Narrow Road" and "Songs of the Bamboo Branches," the titles are song titles of ancient origin for which new words have been provided by the poet. The music that the original songs were presumably set to has been lost.

My introductory essay concentrates on Yüan Hung-tao, the most famous of the Yuan brothers and the one whose writings are most represented in this book. For biographical information on his two brothers Tsung-tao and Chung-tao, see L. Carrington Goodrich and Chaoying Fang, ed., *Dictionary of Ming Biography* (New York and London, 1976), pp. 1637–38.

The illustrations are from the collection of John M. Crawford, Jr. In China there is between poetry and printing a very close relationship that is not present in the West. Poems were often inscribed on paintings for the enhancement of both;

in many instances the subject matter of the two is not directly related, but they work mutually to complement the imagery of each other. Often the poet and the painter are different people. Thus the illustrations in this book come from a variety of sources. Although they may not be directly related to the poetry and prose, they were selected to enhance the writings of the Yüan brothers. Dimensions for the illustrations are given in centimeters; height before width or, in the case of a handscroll, length; dimensions apply to an entire painting, not just a detail.

Once again, I am profoundly indebted to John M. Crawford, Jr., for his generosity in allowing new photographs of art works in his collection to be taken specifically for this book. Some of these works are reproduced here for the first time. Stephen Addiss took the excellent photographs, his sensitive eye picking out the most effective details.

For suggestions that have helped to improve the book immeasurably, I must thank members of the Chinese Poetry Discussion Group, particularly Nathan Sivin, Hung Ming-shui and Kao Yu-kung. Morris Rossabi helped me in my research on the difficult question of Sino-Tibetan relations in the Ming dynasty, and Julian G. Shepherd helped unravel certain entomological problems. To Irving Lo must go the credit for first calling my attention to the riches of Ming poetry.

My wife Anna Caraveli Chaves, to whom this book is dedicated, is a gifted translator of Greek poetry. She has helped iron out several infelicities of expression. But it is her unflagging moral support for which I am especially grateful.

INTRODUCTION

YÜAN HUNG-TAO
AND THE WORLD OF LATE-MING CHINA

There was a time, not so far in the past, when Western admirers of Chinese painting considered the Sung dynasty (960–1279) to be the only great period in the history of the art. The painting of the later dynasties—Yüan (1279–1368), Ming (1368–1644), and Ch'ing (1644–1911)—was seen as derivative and uninteresting. Now, of course, we have come to realize that traditional Chinese painting retained its creativity at least as late as the eighteenth century, a realization made possible by our increasing ability to appreciate the subtleties of Chinese aesthetics. Unfortunately, the same cannot be said for our understanding of Chinese poetry. Although an earlier tendency to concentrate largely on the T'ang dynasty (618–906)—and, to some extent, earlier periods—has more recently given way to an awareness of Sung poetry, the great poets of the three last dynasties remain almost completely unknown. Even many Chinese critics appear to assume that the Yüan, Ming, and Ch'ing dynasties produced nothing in poetry that can compare with earlier achievements. As it happens, this is far from being the case, and we are almost certainly going to witness an expansion of our awareness in this area, as we have already done for painting.

Yüan Hung-tao (1568–1610) was one of the major poets

and essayists of the Ming dynasty, a period that has been described by Charles O. Hueker as "at once the mature culmination of China's ages-old institutional and cultural traditions and, from the opposite point of view, the seedbed from which the institutions and culture of today's China have grown."[1] Yüan's short life (he died at the age of forty-two) falls within the "late Ming" period, which is usually considered to begin with the Wan-li era (1573–1619) and to end with the fall of the dynasty itself in 1644. Yoshitaka Iriya, author of the excellent Japanese book on Yüan Hung-tao, aptly points out that the late Ming was an age of political decadence and confusion, but that from the broader perspective of cultural history it was actually a period of considerable brilliance.[2]

The political and social turmoil that marked these decades is epitomized by the arrogant cruelty of the eunuch Wei Chung-hsien (1568–1627). Born in the same year as Yüan Hung-tao, Wei eventually became a favorite of the governess to the incompetent emperor Hsi Tsung (r. 1620–27). Exercising almost total power, Wei destroyed his enemies ruthlessly until sent into exile himself, whereupon he committed suicide by hanging. His corpse was dismembered by imperial decree, the ultimate degradation in Confucian society.

While the world of the literati was being shaken by the corruption of political power, various complex factors led to the numerous "peasant rebellions" that also characterized the late Ming.[3] Nor were the sufferings of the scholar-officials and those of the Chinese masses completely unrelated. Hueker has described a remarkable demonstration in Suchou (Soochow) against the arrest of a respected official by the agents of Wei Chung-hsien in which both literati and thousands of commoners took part.[4]

It is well known that a time of deep social problems often becomes a time of intense intellectual, religious, and artistic activity. The late Ming was unquestionably such a period. In painting, for example, the research of James Cahill has demonstrated that the extraordinary achievements of the so-called individualist painters of the early Ch'ing dynasty were richly foreshadowed by the late Ming masters, many of whom were downright eccentric. "Conservative and traditional styles were no longer quite respectable,"[5] and the point is amply proved by the exhibition of late Ming painting organized by Cahill in 1971 under the title "The Restless Landscape."[6] Not only was the actual painting of the period innovative, but art historical theory was redefined by the towering figure Tung Ch'i-ch'ang (1555–1636) and his colleagues, Mo Shih-lung and Ch'en Chi-ju.[7]

Yüan Hung-tao was also involved in this development; he was a friend of Tung Ch'i-eh'ang, and in his collected writings he records a conversation with Tung on painting. In the course of this passage, Yüan is moved to reflect: "The good painter learns from things, not from other painters. The good philosopher learns from his mind, not from some doctrine. The good poet learns from the panoply of images, not from writers of the past."[8] Clearly, Yüan sees a basic principle underlying creativity in painting and in poetry, and also philosophy itself. That principle can be described without exaggeration as individualism.

Summarizing late Ming intellectual life, the Japanese scholar Araki Kengo writes: "The most remarkable development in the world of thought in the late Ming was the revival of Buddhism, as it kept pace with the overwhelming popularity of the School of Wang Yang-ming, while at the same time the authority of the School of Chu Hsi rapidly declined."[9] In the sometimes confusing world of what is known as Neo-Confucian thought, Wang Yang-ming (1472–1529) represents an emphasis on the individual mind as opposed to external social norms. Wang felt that each person had within himself an essentially good "intuitive awareness" (*liang-chih*) in which we can all trust. This conception derived ultimately from the classical Chinese philosopher Mencius, but it undoubtedly owed a great deal to Buddhist influence as well, specifically the notion that each individual already has the "Buddha-nature" and need only become aware of it. On the other hand, Chu Hsi (1130–1200), if one can oversimplify his thought, stressed the importance of learning about external "principles" (*li*), and by the Ming dynasty his commentaries on the classics, while masterly in themselves, had come to represent a stultifying orthodoxy. For the school of Wang Yang-ming to triumph in the Wan-li era was for individualism to replace extreme allegiance to tradition in Chinese intellectual life.

This is not to deny the continued presence of those who were outraged by what they regarded as the excessive individualism of some of Wang Yang-ming's later followers. In their view, the most offensive of these was Li Chih (1527–1602). Li called for reliance on one's own intuitions and desires, which he associated with what he called the "childlike mind." He was, not surprisingly, one of Yüan Hung-tao's friends, and Yüan's younger brother, Chung-tao, wrote an important essay on Li Chih.[10] Li, who eventually shaved off his hair and became a kind of unordained Buddhist monk, so incensed his more conservative contemporaries that in 1602 he was arrested and his writings burned. In jail Li committed suicide by cutting his throat.

In such a highly charged environment, it is to be expected that Buddhism would play an important role. Conventional wisdom holds that the anti-Buddhist persecutions of 842–45 permanently ended the main period of creativity in Chinese Buddhist thought, without totally eradicating Buddhism itself. But aside from the splendid Ch'an (Zen) writings of the Sung dynasty, which alone should have raised questions about this view, recent scholarship has shown that the late Ming was a time of considerable Buddhist activity. The central figure was the monk Chu-hung (1535–1615), possibly the major thinker in Chinese Buddhism after the Sung dynasty. Chu-hung's great achievement was the unification of Ch'an Buddhism, oriented toward the practice of meditation leading to revelation of one's innate Buddha-nature, and "Pure Land" Buddhism, which was devotional and called for repetition of the name of Amitabha, the Buddha of the Western Paradise ("Pure Land"), where the devotee would hope to gain rebirth. Chu-hung argued that the mind is the Pure Land, without denying the reality of the Pure Land.[11] In other words, he brought together the intellectual, meditative, and devotional tendencies in Buddhism that had previously developed more or less separately. Chu-hung even debated with one of the first Jesuit missionaries to visit China, Matteo Ricci. (Yüan Hung-tao also knew Ricci, who died in Peking in 1610, the same year as Yüan.) Ricci opposed the Buddhist conception of rebirth and was also against the vegetarianism that Chu-hung championed. He expressed the Christian position that man is the "crown of creation," and that animals were intended for man's benefit.[12]

But Chu-hung was, in the words of a recent writer, "as much a practical missionary as a Buddhist theologian."[13] In this capacity, he became the teacher of Buddhist thought and practice to Yüan Hung-tao and his brothers Tsung-tao and Chung-tao, as well as to such friends of theirs as Yü Ch'un-hsi and T'ao Wang-ling. All these men organized "Clubs for Releasing Life," in which the lay members (i.e., Buddhist believers who would remain laymen without being ordained as monks) would recite Amitabha's name, offer fruit and other things to him, discuss the sutras, and purchase from butchers live animals and then set them free, thus gaining merit.[14] Yüan hung-tao was an enthusiastic follower of Chu-hung, whom he praises in his essay, "A Record of the Hall of Bhaishajyaguru, the Medicine Buddha" (see pp. 89–91). Such pieces as "Discussing the Pure Land with My Friend Fang" (pp. 97–98), and Yüan's other writings on the Pure Land, show the influence of Chu-hung's thought. One of these essays is even included in the *Taisho Tripitaka* (No. 1976), the collected canonical texts of East Asian Buddhism.

At this point we might pause to consider the fact that no

matter which aspect of late Ming intellectual life we have discussed so far—Buddhism, the Wang Yang-ming branch of Neo-Confucianism, and painting and painting theory—we have found that Yuan Hung-tao was a friend of the chief figures involved: Chu-hung, Li Chih, and Tung Ch'i-ch'ang.

YÜAN HUNG-TAO ON LITERATURE

Poetry and poetic theory in the Ming dynasty prior to the time of Yuan Hung-tao were dominated by the so-called Former Seven Masters (*chi'en ch'i tzu*) and Latter Seven Masters (*hou ch'i tzu*).[15] These men, of whom the best known included Li Meng-yang (1473–1579), Li P'an-lung (1514–70), and Wang Shih-chen (1526–90), can be said to have advocated a form of orthodox archaism. They felt that the poetry of the High T'ang masters (Tu Fu, Li Po, Wang Wei et al., all of the eighth century) represented poetic perfection and that a writer of the present age should strive to emulate their styles. Needless to say, such a view was anathema to Yüan Hung-tao, his elder brother Tsung-tao (1560–1600), and their younger brother Chung-tao (1570–1624), who constituted what came to be known as the Kung-an school (after Kung-an Subprefecture, their home town, which was north of Lake Tung-t'ing, in what is now Hupei Province). As Richard John Lynn has written: "The orthodox tradition did not consider poetry to be primarily a medium for the direct expression of individuality and strongly felt emotion, as did the Kung-an school.... It deplored the 'unorthodox' adulation of the self, the ego-centered philosophy of someone like Li Chih—with whose world view people like Yüan Hung-tao…largely concurred."[16] Indeed, Yüan felt strongly that this movement to "restore the past" (*fu-ku*) was misguided. "People speak mistakenly of 'restoring the past': isn't that a big laugh!" He believed that, on the contrary, "as the ways of society undergo change, literature must follow suit."[17] In passage after passage of his letters, Yüan expresses this viewpoint with passionate intensity. Writing to Ch'iu T'an, a close friend, he says:

> In general, things are prized when they are authentic. If I am to be authentic, then my face cannot be the same as your face, and how much less the face of some man of antiquity! The T'ang dynasty had its own poetry—there was no need for the T'ang writers to imitate the style of the *Literary Anthology* [*Wen hsüan*, compiled in the sixth century and representing the major pre-T'ang writers]. And the periods of the T'ang dynasty—Early, High, Middle, and Late—each had *its* own style; there was no need for the whole dynasty to follow its Early and High period writers. Indeed, from Li Po, Tu Fu, Wang Wei, Ts'en Shen, Ch'ien Ch'i, and Liu Ch'ang-ch'ing [all major poets of the T'ang] down to Yüan Chen, Po Chüi, Lu T'ung, and Cheng Ku [later T'ang poets], each man had his own style of poetry. All of them didn't necessarily write just like Li Po and Tu Fu. The Sung dynasty was the same:

did such poets as Ch'en Shih-tao, Ou-yang hsiu, Su Shih, and Huang T'ing-chien [major Sung poets] ever write a single word plagiarized from the T'ang poets? Or a single word plagiarized from each other? In fact, I'd go so far as to say that they *could* not write in the T'ang manner, and that the evolution of the spirit of the age is what made this so. Similarly, the T'ang *could* not have followed the *Literary Anthology* style, and the *Anthology* could not have followed the [earlier] styles of the Han and Wei dynasties.

Now the gentlemen of today wish to "T'ang-ify" the whole world, and they fault the Sung for not having been T'ang in style. Well, if we are going to fault the Sung for not having been the T'ang, why not fault the T'ang for not having been like the *Literary Anthology?* And fault the *Literary Anthology* for not having been like the Han and Wei dynasties? And fault the Han dynasty for not having been like the "Three Hundred Poems" [of the *Book of Songs,* China's most ancient anthology of poetry]? And fault the "Three Hundred Poems" for not having been like the time of "knots in ropes and bird tracks" [i.e., the prehistoric age when messages were conveyed by tying knots in ropes and the earliest writing was being developed by imitating the tracks of birds]? Indeed, wouldn't it be best to make a clean sweep of each and every school of poetry and be left with just a blank sheet of paper![18]

Yüan's forceful satire here calls to mind the contemporary Chilean poet, Nicanor Parra, who writes in his *Letters from the Poet Who Sleeps in a Chair:*

> The poet's duty is this
> To improve on the blank page
> I doubt if it's possible.[19]

Elsewhere, Yüan purposely overstates his case: "People love T'ang poetry. As for me, I say the T'ang dynasty had no poetry. People love Ch'in and Han prose. As for me, I say the Ch'in and Han dynasties had no prose. People denigrate Sung literature and castigate Yüan literature. As for me, I say great poetry and prose will be found precisely in the works of the Sung and Yüan masters!"[20]

But Yüan actually had great admiration for the major T'ang poets, as he makes clear in another letter: "The greatness of the T'ang poets lay in their refusal to model [*wu-fa*] themselves on others.... Although they may have admired other poets, they were utterly unwilling to model their own writings after earlier styles. This is why they transcended all antiquity."[21]

Yüan's use of the term *wu-fa* (lit., "no style," "no method," "without emulating") looks ahead to the famous paradoxical formulation by the early Ch'ing individualist painter Tao-chi (1641–c. 1720): "The method which consists in following no method is the perfect method."[22] Obviously, neither Yüan nor Tao-chi is calling for lack of discipline or for chaos in art. The point is rather that one should follow one's own inner feelings, or "native sensibility" (*hsing-ling*),[23] rather than some external authority.

As Yüan wrote to a friend: "There is no fixed pattern for the expression of newness in literature. You must only put forth something which others could not put forth. The lines, the individual words, the music; each of these must flow out from your own heart. This, truly, is 'newness'."[24] This passage is as close as one can come in traditional Chinese criticism to a conception of individualism as a principle of artistic creativity. Great writers of the past, such as the T'ang masters, were successful because they were true to their inner selves, not because they blindly followed some predetermined model. The parallel here to Wang Yang-ming's emphasis on "intuitive awareness" should be obvious.

Yüan Hung-tao's view of literature led him, as might be expected, to find literary value in unusual places. While he certainly admired many of the established poets, particularly the great Sung master Su Shih (Su Tung-p'o, 1037–1101), Yüan shared with Li Chih and the remarkable critic Chin Sheng-t'an (d. 1661) the opinion that fiction, drama, and even folk songs (or what would now be called, more accurately, oral poetry) must be seen as serious literature as well. In the traditional scheme, Chinese "novels" and plays were barely tolerated as entertainment; they certainly did not qualify as high art, on the same level with classical poetry, essays, historical writings and the like. And folk songs per se were almost totally neglected, although Confucian theory held that many poems in the *Book of*

Songs originated among the "people." (These, and later *yüeh-fu* poems, were probably edited and redacted, although to what extent remains a matter of controversy.) But Yüan Hung-tao was a friend and admirer of one of the greatest Ming playwrights, T'ang Hsien-tsu (1550–1616), and in a list of his own favorite reading, Yüan casually mentions the great novel *Shui-hu chuan* (*Walter Margin,* translated by Pearl Buck as *All Men Are Brothers*) and the plays of the Yüan dynasty (the golden age of Chinese drama) side by side with the poetry of Tu Fu and the *Records of the Historian* by Ssu-ma Ch'ien (145?–90? b.c.), China's most respected work of historiography![25] The emotional impact of such a juxtaposition at the time would be even greater than if a professor of English literature were to announce today that his favorite authors were Milton, Shakespeare, and the script writers for the television series "Kojak" (much greater, in fact, as a kind of reverse snobbery has made it fashionable in certain academic circles to praise television programs). Yüan also enjoyed hearing a master storyteller named Chu recite episodes of *Shui-hu chuan* orally, presumably improvising upon them in the age-old manner. In a poem on Chu's performance, he even claims that he prefers *Shui-hu chuan* to the Six Confucian Classics and the writings of Ssu-ma Ch'ien, a statement calculated to infuriate more traditionally minded scholars.[26] It is small wonder that Yüan's writings were officially proscribed in the Ch'ien-lung era (1736–96), along with the works of many others considered to constitute a threat to public morality!

As for folk songs, Yüan proclaims:

> In our age there is no literature,
> but in the village alleys
>> there are real poems![27]

In one of his most important essays, he develops this thought further. Most contemporary writing will not endure, Yüan says, because it is blindly imitative of earlier works. But the songs sung by village women and children are a different matter: "These are composed by real people, so they have real resonance! They are not slavish imitations of the Han and Wei dynasties, they do not follow in the footsteps of the High T'ang period. They are produced naturally, from the inner nature, and they express human happiness, anger, grief, joy, love, and desire. This is what makes them worth savoring."[28] Here again, Yüan happens to be in the vanguard of an important movement of his time. Very shortly after Yüan's death, the famous writer and editor of vernacular fiction Feng Meng-lung (1574–1646) published his *Shan-ko* (Mountain Songs), "probably the earliest collection of Chinese songs in pure colloquial form."[29] It might be noted that it is only in recent years that the artistic value of oral poetry has come to be fully appreciated even in the West.[30]

Yüan was also able to recognize the artistry of the Chinese shadow-puppet theater, a form of popular theater widely disseminated and still performed in countries such as Indonesia, Thailand, Turkey, and Greece. He was inspired to write a group of three poems on the subject, in one of which he says:

They may not have bones or sinews,
but they have spirit![31]

Yüan Hung-tao the Writer

There is no need to recount Yüan's life here in detail, as C.N. Tay has done so in a readily available source.[32] We may note that Yüan obtained the *chin-shih* degree (a kind of Ph.D. enabling one to enter the official bureaucracy) in 1592 and held various government posts during his life. While performing the duties of magistrate of Wu-hsien (Suchou), he wrote to his friends:

> It's not that I'm *unwilling* to be an official, but I can't help feeling that it simply runs against the grain of my heart! . . .;
>
> Being an official entails suffering; being a magistrate causes the most suffering of all. And if you're magistrate of Wu-hsien, then the suffering is multiplied a million-fold, worse than the labors of ox or horse. Why? Because superiors visit you like gathering clouds, travelers stop by like drops of rain, papers pile up like mountains, an ocean of taxes in cash or grain must be collected: if you work and write morning and night, you still can't keep up with all of it! Misery, misery![33]

Far more interesting to Yüan were the literary gatherings of the Grape Society (*P'u-t'ao she*) that he and his brothers founded at the Ch'ung-kuo Temple of Peking in 1598; his Buddhist activities, centering around the monk Chu-hung; and, perhaps most important of all, the many journeys he made to the magnificent mountains of China. These journeys inspired Yüan's superb travel essays (several are translated here), which influenced in turn the better-known travelogues of the great explorer Hsü hsia-k'o (1586–1641). Although Yüan's travels were not as extensive as Hsü's, it is clear from his travel essays that he often went beyond the frequently climbed paths to clamber up cliff faces or to crawl through caves. Yüan was searching for new experiences in nature, partly in the hope that these would breathe new life into his poetry.

Another form of exploration led Yüan to seek out kindred spirits among the writers of the past. The archaists were calling for unthinking emulation of one or two poets, but Yüan kept an open mind. His rediscovery of the poetry of Hsü Wei (1521–93) is well known. One night, while looking through the books at the home of his friend T'ao Wang-ling, he came across a dusty old volume of poetry: "I read some of it in the lamplight. Before I had gotten through just a few poems, I found myself jumping with amazement. I shouted out to T'ao, 'Who is this? A contemporary? An old master?' T'ao replied: 'This is a book by Mr. Hsü Wei, a native of my district.'"[34]

Yüan's enthusiasm is not hard to understand. Here was a relatively recent poet who was writing the kind of imaginative, expressive poetry Yüan himself favored. Although best known today as a painter, calligrapher, and playwright, Hsü Wei is indeed a most interesting poet. One of Hsü's characteristic poems expresses an idea thoroughly in keeping with Yüan's philosophy:

> I ONCE DID A BAMBOO PAINTING FOR SOMEBODY—
> NOW HE WANTS ME TO DO ANOTHER, AND
> I HAVE WRITTEN THIS TO ANSWER HIM.
>
> This bamboo I painted a long time ago.
> Now you want me to do another?—Impossible!
> When the sparrow grows old
>   it becomes a clam in the sea.
> You ask it to turn back into a sparrow,
>   but how can it fly again?[35]

Not only is it unfair to ask an artist to repeat what others have done, it is wrong even to expect him to repeat himself!

Like Hsü Wei, Yüan Hung-tao has been remembered less for his poetry than for his other achievements. Yüan's literary theory (shared by his brothers) is so striking in itself that there is a tendency to discuss the Kung-an school for its polemical position and to ignore the actual poetry of Yüan Hung-tao, Yüan Tsung-tao, and Yüan Chung-tao.[36] Frequently, Yüan Hung-tao's admittedly bizarre poem "West Lake" (see p. 62) is the sole example quoted, and is used to demonstrate the sheer weirdness of Kung-an poetry. This is unfair, as virtually no other poem of Yüan's can be called weird, at least in the same sense as this one. In addition, Yüan's essays and other prose pieces (or *hsino-p'in-wen*—a number are translated here) are also so remarkable that they too tend to overshadow the poems. Consequently, Yüan's poetry has attracted little attention.[37]

In my opinion, a careful reading of Yüan's poetry reveals him to be the single greatest poet of the Ming dynasty, more inventive even than Kao Ch'i (1336–74), to whom this title would be granted by most. Despite his polemics against imitation of the past, Yüan is not afraid to write on traditional themes. But he does so in such a way as to apply these themes to his own expressive needs. For example, the poem "Twenty-first Day of the Seventh Month" (p. 82) draws heavily on the rich imagery and impressionistic atmosphere of innumerable poems on the ancient "neglected wife" themes. as well as on the elegiac tone of laments for the dead (*tao-wang*), but Yüan leaves his sources far behind. Not only does the poem appear to modulate from the third person to the first person of the man (rather than the woman, as was traditional), but the gentle melancholy of the neglected-wife poems gives way to real passion. This passion is not expressed explicitly, but rather (through the most surreal use of imagery and the kinds of imaginative leaps—between past and present, concrete and abstract, waking and dreaming—that one expects of a Lorca or a Neruda. The last four lines of the poem are a triumphant synthesis of all these levels.

Similarly, in "Making Fun of Myself on People Day" (p. 39), the poet purposely takes upon himself every available stereotyped role in Chinese literati society, while avoiding precisely the actions which are most characteristic of those roles. He is an official who does not wear official robes, a farmer who does not plow his fields, a Confucian scholar who does not read books, a Taoist hermit who delights in sensuality. The idea is developed in increasingly exciting imagery of liberation, until two classical allusions bring the poem back down to earth.

Yuan has a number of poems in which the everyday lives of the common people he so admired are beautifully evoked. He creates as rich a tapestry as the storytellers who produced *Shui-hu chuan* and the other early novels:

> Village women, speaking with a trace
> of a southern accent . . .

> A little boy . . . shouts:
> "I am the King of the Bull Fights!"

> The boatwoman. . .
> her left hand steadies a little girl,
> her right works the rudder . . .

> The girl is from Shansi, a turban on her head,
> face heavy with make-up, hair thick with grease.

In his prose writings too, Yüan creates successful vignettes of life in realms of society that were rarely depicted in classical Chinese literature. A letter to one of his uncles offers a rare glimpse of living conditions among the urban poor: "Tsung

Ping (375-443) has said: 'I have found that riches are not as good as poverty and high position not as good as low.' At first, I used to think this was a pretentious statement. But now I believe it. Once I said to Huang Hui [1554 TO 612]: 'Just look in the old temples and cold shops along the streets of Ch'ang-an at midnight: there the beggar boys and mendicant monks are snoring away like thunder. Meanwhile, the white-haired old millionaires are huddled among their silken blankets, behind their bed curtains, wishing in vain for just a moment of shut-eye!'"[38]

Yüan's powers of observation, evident in this passage and in the poems on everyday life, become most acute in his extraordinary essays on insects, "Raising Crickets," "Ant Fights," and "Spider Fights" (see pp. 99-107). Dr. Julian Shepherd, an entomologist at the State University of New York at Binghamton, was kind enough to go over my translations of these essays with me. He was particularly impressed by "Ant Fights," which he described as "very accurate." He further pointed out that the discipline of socio-biology, which only dates back twenty or so years, has stressed the study of communication among ants, which depend not upon sight cues but rather upon olfactory cues for which their antennae are the most important "sensory modality." Dr. Shepherd was struck by Yüan Hung-tao's apparent understanding of this concept. Similarly, Yüan's observations on spider fights are so precise that it was no surprise to read recently in the *New York Times* of "boys [in Singapore] who comb the fields for large spiders to be pitted against each other in fights to the death in circles traced in the dirt—small coins hinging on the breathlessly awaited outcome."[39]

There is no question in my mind that Yüan's poems and essays (which can be regarded as prose poems of a sort) retain today the liveliness and expressiveness that set them apart three hundred and fifty years ago from the dry, academic exercises of many of his contemporaries.

NOTES

1. Charles O. Hucker, ed., *Chinese Government in Ming Times* (New York and London, 1969), p. vi.

2. Yoshitaka Iriya, *En Kōdō* [Yüan Hung-tao], Chugoku shijin senshu, series 2, vol. 11 (Tokyo, 1963), introduction, p. 1.

3. Charles O. Hucker, *Two Studies in Ming History*, Michigan Papers in Chinese Studies, no. 12 (University of Michigan, 1971), p. 41.

4. *Ibid*, pp. 41–67.

5. James Cahill, "Wu Pin and His Landscape Painting," *Proceedings of the International Symposium on Chinese Painting* (National Palace Museum, Taipei, 1970), p. 641.

6. See the catalogue, James Cahill, T*he Restless Landscape: Chinese Painting of the Late Ming Period* (University Art Museum, Berkeley, 1971).

7. For details, see Fu Shen, "A Study of the Authorship of the 'Huashuo,'" *Proceedings of the International Symposium*, pp. 85–110; and Nelson I. Wu, "Tung Ch'i-ch'ang: Apathy in Government and Fervor in Art," in Arthur F. Wright and Denis Twitchett, ed., Confucian Personalities (Stanford, 1962), pp. 260–93.

8. WC (see Bibliographical Note for this and other abbreviations). See also Mae Anna Quan Pang, "Late Ming Painting Theory," in Cahill, T*he Restless Landscape*, pp. 23–24.

9. Araki, Kengo, "Confucianism and Buddhism in the Late Ming," in William

Theodore deBary and the Conference on Seventeenth-Century Chinese Thought, *The Unfolding of Neo-Confucianism* (New York and London, 1975), p. 39.

10. For a thorough discussion of Li Chih, and many of the issues raised here, see William Theodore deBary, "Individualism and Humanitarianism in Late Ming Thought," in deBary, ed., *Self and Society in Ming Thought* (New York and London, 1970), pp. 188–225.

11. Leon Hurvitz, "Chu-hung's One Mind of Pure Land and Ch'an Buddhism," in deBary, *Self and Society,* pp. 451–79.

12. For a detailed account, see Kristin Yü Greenblatt, "Chu-hung and Lay Buddhism in the Late Ming," in deBary et al., *The Unfolding,* pp. 113-16.

13. *Ibid.,* p. 110.

14. *Ibid.,* pp. 110-11.

15. For the best discussion of these writers in English, see Richard John Lynn, "Orthodoxy and Enlightenment: Wang Shih-chen's Theory of Poetry and Its Antecedents," in deBary et al., T*he Unfolding,* pp. 217-66.

16. *Ibid.,* p. 255.

17. *CT,* p. 37.

18 *Ibid.,* pp. 19-20.

19. Nicanor Parra, *Emergency Poems,* trans. Miller Williams (New York, 1972), p. 27. Reprinted by permission of New Directions Pub. Corp.

20. *CT,* p. 34.

21. *Ibid.,* p. 43.

22. As translated by Osvald Sirén and quoted in Richard Edwards, T*he Painting of Tao-chi* (Ann Arbor, 1967), p. 23.

23. James J. Y. Liu's translation of the term, in *The Art of Chinese Poetry* (Chicago, 1962), p. 74. The term is used by Yüan Hung-tao, e.g., *WC,* p. 10.

24. *CT,* p. 57.

25. *YC,* p. 11. Yüan is clearly being facetious when he complains that he has long since grown tired of all these books.

26. *SC,* p. 21. See also *YC,* p. 11.

27. *SC,* p. 40.

28. *WC,* p. 6.

29. John McCoy, review of Cornelia Töpelmann, *Shan-ko von Feng Menglung: Eine Volksliedersammlung aus der Ming-Zeit, Harvard Journal of Asiatic Studies,* vol. 36 (1976), p. 305. McCoy says that the first publication of Shan-ko probably took place between 1610 and 1619 (p. 303, note).

30. See especially Albert Lord, *The Singer of Tales* (New York, 1968; originally pub-

lished 1960); and Ruth Finnegan, *Oral Poetry* (Cambridge, 1977).

31. *SC*, pp. 164-65.

32. C. N. Tay, entry on Yüan Hung-tao, in L. Carrington Goodrich and Chaoying Fang, ed., *Dictionary of Ming Biography* (New York and London, 1976), pp. 1635-38.

33. *CT*, p. 10 for the two letters quoted here.

34 *WC*, p 1.

35. *Hsü Wen-ch'ang san chi* (National Central Library reprint, Taipei, 1968), p. 881. The last two lines refer to a passage in the *Monthly Ordinances* (Yüeh ling) of the classic *Book of Rites:* "In the last month of autumn, the sparrow enters the great ocean to become a clam."

36. Yüan's brothers, Tsung-tao and Chung-tao, are also fine poets, and some representative works of theirs are included here..

37. A more balanced picture is presented by Yang Te-pen in his recent book *Yüan Chung-lang wen-hsüeh ssu-hsiang* [The Literary Thought of Yüan Hung-tao] (Taipei, 1976). See also the Japanese anthology of Yüan's poetry referred to in note 2.

38. *CT*, p. 64.

39. David A. Andelman, "In Restrictive Singapore, Gambling Serves as Safety Valve," *The New York Times*, February 5, 1977.

Shen Chou (1427–1509): "Silent Angler in an Autumn Wood" (detail). Hanging scroll, ink and colors on paper, 149.9 x 61 cm.

Tao-chi (1641–c. 1720): "Drunk in Autumn Woods." Hanging scroll, ink and colors on paper, 160 x 69.6 cm.

POEMS BY YÜAN HUNG-TAO

Leaving Po-hsiang at Dawn

I get out of bed before sunrise
and, half asleep, climb into my carriage.
These official journeys are like food stuck in the teeth,
homesickness as unpalatable as spoiled water chestnuts!
A girl stands in front of an inn, her hair uncombed.
A Buddhist monk boils water in a little hut.
Not intoxicated, but not sober either,
I listen as the morning drum sounds through the dust.

On Receiving My Letter of Termination

The time has come to devote myself to my hiker's stick;
I must have been a Buddhist monk in a former life!
Sick, I see returning home as a kind of pardon.
A stranger here—being fired is like being promoted.
In my cup, thick wine; I get crazy-drunk,
eat my fill, then stagger up the green mountain.
The southern sect, the northern sect, I've tried them all:
this hermit has his own school of Zen philosophy.

A Playful Poem on Seeing a Rubbing of Some of My Poetry at Ting-chou

In the pagoda—an ink rubbing of my verses!
Whoever engraved them here?
They fill the air, like the chirping of a worm;
cover the wall—calligraphy like insects!
Sooner or later, they'll be eaten away by the moss
or effaced by the wind and rain.
But for now, my poems have been cut in stone:
my seal-vermilion drips to the ground below.

[The rubbing would be made from a stone engraving. Paper would be placed over the stone, and ink pressed carefully against the paper. A seal might be applied, using vermilion ink.]

ON MEETING MY ELDER BROTHER UPON ARRIVING
IN THE CAPITAL—A POEM ON HIS RECENT LIFE

You have turned your back on the busy crowds of the world
and chant to yourself from secondhand books.
Your official post is not important—
        you have few contacts with people;
a long stay in the capital has brought new wrinkles to
        your face.
On the cracked walls are portraits of Buddhist monks;
high in the windows, birds' nests can be seen.
Editor at the Academy—not the greatest job,
but still, be careful of the wind and waves!

Making Fun of Myself on "People Day"

Seventh day of the first month.

This official wears no official sash,
this farmer pushes no plow,
this Confucian does not read books,
this recluse does not live in the wilds.
In society, he wears lotus leaves for clothes,
among commoners, he is decked out in cap and jade.
His serenity is achieved without closing the door,
his teaching is done without instruction.
This Buddhist monk has long hair and whiskers,
this Taoist immortal makes love to beautiful women.
One moment, withering away in a silent forest,
the next, bustling through crowds on city streets.
When he sees flowers, he calls for singing girls;
when he has wine to drink, he calls for a pair of dice.
His body is as light as a cloud
floating above the Great Clod.
Try asking the bird, flying in the air:
"What clear pond reflects your image?"
How free! the dragon, curling, leaping,
liberated! beyond this world, or in it.
The official, Liu-hsia Hui, firm, yet harmonious;
or Hermit Yi, pure in his retirement.

Rising from My Sickbed, I Saw the Moon as the Sky Cleared

This was the night of the midautumn moon of the year i-ssu [1605].

Up from my sickbed, I meet the full moon—
the clouds open, a smile opens on my face.
The clouds depart with what's left of my depression;
the moon appears with the new good feelings.
Falling leaves are iced with clear dew,
new fragrance rises from the thick wine.
This gladness is still not deep in my heart,
but these are embers, ready to burst into flame.

I Get Up from My Sickbed and Sit by Myself

The wild grass—green and misty;
has there ever been an autumn that did not bring pain?
This sick man's house has no visitors—
even my little dog sleeps all day.
I must look in books for things to use in poems;
no money for wine to warm me up, I put on extra clothes.
The door shut, I read Chuang Tzu:
the chapters on "Horses' Hoofs" and the "Floods of
        Autumn."

DREAMING

The dream world cannot be found
        away from my pillow—
but nowhere on the pillow can I find it.
And when I am in the dream world
my pillow might as well not exist.
Awake, I feel my dreams are empty;
in dream, the waking world has disappeared.
Can I be sure that the waking universe
has no pillow beneath it?
If dream and waking alternate,
which is fantasy, which is real?

THE FIRST DAY OF SPRING—ON GOLD OX ROAD

This is the day the farmer puts down his plow,
the young girl leaves her loom,
the scholar sets aside his books,
the official stops collecting taxes,
the merchant closes shop,
the fisherman hauls in his nets . . .
So why am I the only man
walking dangerous slopes, under towering mountains?

RETURNING HOME AT NIGHT FROM HSIEN-LING SHRINE

Storm clouds gather—dark, like cast iron;
beating my clothes, striking my face: hot particles of
     sand.
Darkness like splashed ink covers roads and avenues;
windblown lamps flutter on and off like ghosts.
"Bong! Bong!"—I hear a temple bell
and run in to share the monks' blankets of paper.
Tiles and beams rain down from the roof;
the Thunder God loses control of his chariot,
     the wheels break up.
A great wind sweeps the ground, opens the sky;
one star shines through, above the cloudbanks.
Once again, my horse's hoofs fight against the blast;
no torches lighting the way, the long road is narrow.
Lightning flashes through the sky—a display of beautiful
     silks!
Some threads are fine, like a dancing girl's hair,
     some thick as a rope.
Clouds, mountains, flowers, birds—each design suggested,
but the threads fly too fast for the Sky Maiden to weave
     anything.
People say a flash of lightning is a smile of heaven—
what is it that amuses the Lord of Heaven so much?
The Moon Goddess hides, the Weaving Girl disappears;
why is this dumb darkness covering everything?
Now, outside Pei-an Gate, water covers the road,

raindrops are falling on the roofs and on the trees.
Amazing!—on one side of the road the sky is cloudy,
        on the other, clear,
as if the Rain God were trying to protect me.
I make it back home—no lights are on;
I yell at my servants to boil up some hot gruel.
As I dash off my poem—ink covering the Wu paper—
the last raindrops splatter lightly on the bamboo
        beneath the eaves.

The "Slowly, Slowly" Poem

Playfully inscribed on the wall.

The bright moon slowly, slowly rises,
the green mountains slowly, slowly descend.
The flowering branches slowly, slowly redden,
the spring colors slowly, slowly fade.
My salary slowly, slowly increases,
my teeth slowly, slowly fall out,
my lover's waist slowly, slowly expands,
my complexion slowly, slowly ages.

We are low in society
        in the days of our greatest health,
our pleasure comes when we are no longer young.
The Goddess of Good Luck
        and the Dark Lady of Bad Luck
are with us every step we take.
Even heaven and earth are imperfect
and human society is full of ups and downs.
Where do we look for real happiness?
—Bow humbly, and ask the Masters of Taoist Arts.

A Record of My Trip to Mount She

I.

Yellow leaves spiral down through the air;
waterfall spray flies into raindrops.
Patches of moss darken Buddha's face;
the stones here have been brushed by the robes of a god.
The monks are tranquil, though their kitchen has few
        vegetables;
the mountain, cold—not many sparrows in the flock.
Of themselves, my worries all disappear;
I do not have to try to forget the world.

2.

Height after height of strange mountain scenes,
new words, new ideas in our conversation.
Wild pines blow in the wind like hanging manes;
the ancient rocks are covered with mottled scales.
I enter the temple, seek the dream realm of the monks,
thumb through sutras, feel the dustiness of this traveler's life.
You, the Zen master, I, a lover of wine—
we are brothers, way beyond the people of the world.

TRAVELING THROUGH HUAI-AI BY BOAT

Three hundred miles along the canal;
ten thousand willow branches, my broken heart.
Travel is the root of sorrow, clings to it like glue;
meditation—that is that way to control this suffering.
Homesick, I think about fish-on-rice;
drunk, I dream about clam chowder . . .
More and more, too lazy to study books,
spider webs covering my brush rack.

[This poem is one from a group of four.]

Passing Through Suchou in the Rain

Out of a job, with roads to travel, still stuck here in Wu—
could it be this T'ao Ch'ien is a lazy pedant after all?
My soul seeks flowers, as if it were a butterfly,
or follows the waves in dreams, like a pelican.
A lonely lamp, skinny shadow—Cold Mountain Temple;
wild grass, flowing green—Hsia-chia Lake.
I've studied Tao, practiced Zen, and gotten nowhere:
now I'm like Yang Chu, who wouldn't give anyone a single
      hair off his head.

[This poem is one from a set of two. T'ao Ch'ien was the great Chin-dynasty poet who quit his job as a government official. Yang Chu was a philosopher of the mid-fourth century B.C. whose philosophy was misinterpreted as hedonism by some and selfishness by others (see A. C. Graham, *The Book of Lieh-tzu*, London, 1960, pp. 135ff. and 148-49).]

Getting Up in the Morning
After Staying Overnight at Huan-chu Temple

Hey there, Yüan Hung-tao !
Why not get up with the crack of dawn?
A hundred thousand universes
        have been blown by the wind
into an ocean of cloud.
 —I throw on my clothes,
        go out and take a look:
sure enough, the clouds are stretched out below.
The whole sky is filled with crystal forms—
such is the power of the mountain god!

SAYING GOODBYE TO THE MONK WU-NIEN

Each five years we meet
then grieve when we must part.
It has taken only three farewells
for fifteen years to pass.
I recall how I tried to study meditation with you
but I was like the yellow poplar
      which grows for a while
            then shrinks again.
A hundred times I heard you lecture
but my mind remained a tangled knot.
I was like a man born blind
who has never seen red or purple—
try explaining the difference to him
and the more you speak
      the more confused he'll get.
I can't bear to leave you now
but it is impossible for us
      to stay together.
It is October—the river winds are blowing hard;
please let your hair grow back in
      to protect your head from the cold.

I Went Out at Night With the Monk Liao. We Went to
Wang's For Drinks. When the Wine Had Been Served, a
Great Thunderstorm Started Up. Everyone Else Flinched
With Fright but I Felt Wonderful. The Storm Went On
until After Midnight.

Heaven is in a dark, ugly mood—
rumbling thunder, driving wind and rain.
Books tumble off the desk, into storage jars;
the children run and hide under their beds.
And Master Shan?—He slams his fist on the table,
         shouts out loud,
wets his whistle cup of rhinoceros horn
and walks home
         without a candle
flashes of red lightning
         lighting his way.

Tung Ch'i-ch'ang (1555–1636): "Landscape with Trees and Pavilion: (detail).
Hanging scroll, ink on paper, 95 x 42.4 cm.

Mo Shih–lung (c. 1550–c. 1585): "Landscape" (detail). Handscroll, ink and colors on paper, 80.6 x 21 cm.

On The Way to Yü-ch'ien

I left home two, three months ago—
the traveler's life is one long climb!
Ask me—I don't know myself
why I'm running around.
The southern birds make fun of me;
they say: "Old man go back!"
And why shouldn't this old man go back?
All these mountains are making me sick.
Every hundred *li* another famous mountain
that takes ten days to see.
The southeast is a land of cliffs
and I haven't covered one-tenth of it.
Each morning, clouds touch my eyebrows;
every night, mountain demons enter my room.
I meet people, ask about techniques of meditation
or the art of levitation, if they are immortals.
Every bone in my body aches
but in many ways my spirit is free.
You can come to the end of the World's famous sights
but the wanderer's inspiration is hard to subdue.

Poet's note: The southerners call the cuckoo "Old-Man-Go-Back"

CHRYSANTHEMUMS IN WINTER

There are no flowers that never fade,
yet here are the chrysanthemums,
      still blooming in winter.
To protect their leaves, I weave a bamboo trellis;
to keep them fragrant, cut away the weeds.
Now, chilling our hearts, the cold breaks upon us;
old friends come, bringing wine.
Suddenly, we remember the old man of the eastern hedge,
chant his poems out loud, raise our cups in a toast.

[The old man of the eastern hedge: T'ao Ch'ien (365-427), famous for his love of chrysanthemums. His best known couplet on the subject is: "I pluck chrysanthemums beneath the eastern hedge, / and, in the distance, see the southern mountains."]

Poem Written at Willow Lake

At sunset, I lie down for a nap—
the mountains seem to tumble onto my pillow.
Green mosses are reflected in the water;
winds from the rice field blow through the window.
I enjoy myself here, arranging rocks and flowers
       in the garden,
writing out spells to keep away crows and bugs.
My drinking companions are mostly Buddhist monks;
even when we're drunk, we talk about the Void.

[This poem is one from a group of three. A friend gave Willow Lake to Yüan
Hung-tao in exchange for a Buddhist statue.]

Drinking at the Studio of Fang Wei-chin

There are many pleasures to be enjoyed
       at your studio:
we play chess, have a drinking contest . . .
The waters of the Wei lap the walls;
we see the reflections of sailing boats
       in the wine jug.
Fish hawks peer down at your brush rack;
riverside flowers fall among the chessmen.
We roll up a curtain, meet new poems,
chant them out loud as we look
       at the catalpa trees.

TRAVELING BY BOAT TO GOLD HARBOR—
DRINKING WITH SAN-MU AND WANG HUI

How happy I feel in the country!
All along the riverbank—flowers on the hedges.
Old farmers sit in the fields, crushing lice;
river girls lie with their fishing poles, asleep.
The households in this little harbor
       pay their taxes in reeds;
the granary holds rice duties
       collected from the barges.
We have a boat and some fresh wine to drink—
this happiness has nothing to do with money!

I Recently bought a Fancy Boat That I Plan to Make My Home, so I Have Written a Series of Poems on Living in a Boat

I plan to make this boat my peaceful home,
under the moon, following the wind
          wherever it may lead.
The fish and waterbirds?
          I'll ask them to be my secretaries.
The clouds and mist will hire me as their scribe.
I'll live here like a wood grub,
          deep within the tree,
and travel like the snail,
          who carries his own home.
Beneath me—not a strip of land;
          above—not one roof tile.
From this day on, I entrust my body
          to the elements.

[This poem is one from a group of ten.]

Watching the Boat Races at the Dragon Boat Festival, the year Shen-ch'en (1604)

I.

The lake, newly swelled, is slippery as oil;
red banners, a hundred feet long, flutter past the trees.
I have two or three pieces of old, coarse silk:
I'll tear them into strips to tie at the prow of my boat.

2.

From Pi-han Tower, the water fills the valley.
At Cho-tsu Pond, the sun sinks in the west.
On the bridge, below the bridge—people like ants;
I only hope Duke Meng Embankment does not collapse
        under the weight.

Hsin-an River

The waves here are bad,
        the head winds are terrible;
the foliage, all green—even the rocks are green.
From dark cliffs we hear
        the murmuring of ghosts,
wild fires wake dragons with their heat.
The trees are old—from T'ang-dynasty stock;
the steles, toppled over,
        bear Sung-dynasty inscriptions.
Stepping ashore, we meet an old farmer
who claims that ape men inhabit these woods.

[This poem is one from a group of ten.]

ON BOARD A BOAT AT CHI-NING

The mouth of the Wen River—240 feet wide,
a torrent like a cliff of water, all the way across.
In one night, the wind that blows the grain boats
        from the south
has swept us as far as the Nan-wang locks.
How many days since I left home?
In an instant, months and months have passed!
Traveling by canal, there's been no fixed schedule
but now we should be one stage from Peking.
For a hundred *li*—a storm of yellow sand
in a dry wind that sounds like ripped cloth.

I've long since been competing for a place at the table;
my body feels sullied by the muddy waves.
Thirty years old, and what have I accomplished?
Strive, strive—for a cluster of empty hopes.
Compare me to a boat, struggling upstream,
which gains one foot, and then loses two.

"Songs of the Bamboo Branches"

1.

At the mouth of the Lung-chou River
  the water looks like sky:
here the women of Lung-chou operate the great boats.
Waves splashing her face, one of them asks the traveler,
"Are you scared? Watch my boat list
  under eight feet of wind!"

2.

The boatwoman has painted eyebrows.
Her boat is like a leaf, following the waves of the river.
Her left hand steadies a little girl,
  her right works the rudder,
and her dark hair, piled high as a mountain,
  stays perfectly in place.

Poet's note: This is a description of what I actually saw.

[These are two poems from a group of twelve.]

WEST LAKE

One day I walk by the lake.
One day I sit by the lake.
One day I stand by the lake.
One day I lie by the lake.

[This poem is one from a set of two.]

AFTER READING CHI-TIEN'S POEMS ON WEST LAKE

How many times
        have I stepped alone
                into the boat at West Lake?
The boatman knows me now
        and never asks for money.
One note sung by a bird
        breaks the total silence—
it sounds from the mountain
        that slants below
                the setting sun.

[This poem is one from a group of four. Chi-tien was possibly Tao-chi (d. 1209), a Buddhist monk of the Sung dynasty.]

At White Deer Spring

A little fishpond just over two feet square,
and not terribly deep.
A pair goldfish swim in it
as freely as in a lake.
Like bones of mountains among icy autumn clouds
tiny stalagmites pierce the rippling surface.
For the fish, it is a question of being alive—
they don't worry about the depth of the water.

Improvised on the Road

In the second month I returned to my home town.
In the fourth month—back on the road again.
Children gaze at me in the narrow lanes;
across the steam, a scholar laughs out loud.

[This poem is one from a group of three.]

Improvised on the Road

He rides a thoroughbred, with bridle of red silk.
He wears an official cap, and a robe
      embroidered with gold dragons.
A little boy runs out into the road,
      blocks his way, and shouts:
"I am the King of the Bull Fights!"

[This poem is one from a group of six.]

Things Experienced

Green leaves start to wither on the trees;
white waves sweep across the river.
People gossip of invasions in the east;
rumors fly: "We've sent ships from the north!"
I buy some Ch'ü-chou oranges, spotted with frost;
listen all day to famous women singers.
There are many marriage ceremonies here in Yang-chou—
flutes and drums play loud as night draws on.

[Yoshitaka Iriya considers the third and fourth lines to refer to Hideyoshi's
notorious invasion of Korea in 1592; the Chinese did in fact dispatch ships with
troops and food to aid the Korean cause.]

WRITING DOWN WHAT I SEE

The setting sun brings a pallor to the face of autumn;
floating clouds gather quickly into clusters.
They slant down, veiling the trees,
only two or three mountains still visible in the haze.
My horse glances back at the bridge-spanned river;
a group of monks returns along a path of pine trees.
The cliff is too high—I can see no temple;
suddenly, through the mist, I hear
        a temple bell.

*On the Eighteenth Day of the twelfth month, I arrived at Ch'i-yang and left
my boat. From Hsing-kuo I traveled to Hsien-ning, taking a route that
emerged at Gold Ox Commandery. The mountain road was like the blade of
a knife; whirling snow froze the skin, and the sedan-chair bearers were so mis-
erable they could hardly walk. But there were mountains everywhere covered
with snow—some like crows' necks, others like piles of jewels. This is indeed
one of the pleasures of traveling. Along the way, I improvised poems on the
things I saw, and ended up with sixteen quatrains.*

    3.

Wild bamboo, roots clutching the rocks:
village women, speaking with a trace
        of a southern accent . . .
The guide points ahead and says to me:
"That's Little Fork Mountain up there !"

9.

Don't be upset that the horses' hoofs are sinking.
Don't worry because the cart wheels are stuck in mud.
Imagine if you were alone here with your walking stick,
trudging through the snow to look at the mountains!

12.

Peak after peak, dotted with snow;
bend after bend, cold mountain stream—
I have a feeling of déjà vu;
in a painting by Wang Wei I've seen this place before.

13.

A man is walking along a craggy ridge;
his head appears above a cliff, then disappears again.
A horse descends a bridge across a stream
and suddenly is swallowed by the snow.

16.

RESTING AT SSU-CHO TEMPLE

The temple is at Gold Ox Commandery

Pigs tied to the throne of the Heavenly King;
birds nesting in the cap of the Great Judge.
Chickens perch here,
        and make a market of their own;
wood from a deer pen forms the gate.

[These are five poems from a group of sixteen.]

"IN CH'ANG-AN THERE IS A NARROW ROAD"

She reins in her horse,
stands by the watering trough.
Loquats falling—it is autumn—
        dogwood in bloom.
The girl is from Shansi, a turban on her head,
face heavy with make-up, hair thick with grease.
She plays the zither of twenty-five strings
and wears a gown of scarlet with purple threads.
Smiling, she asks:
        "Is this how they dress down south?"

On the Twenty-third Day I arrived at P'u-ch'i. Inspector Hsieh came out to welcome me. At the time he was ninety-two. With his hair like crane feathers and his ruddy complexion, he could still ride horses and drive chariots—truly a treasure among men. I improvised these two poems to commemorate the splendor of the occasion.

I.

A parade of banners and insignia—
　　　　thousands of people crowd around
to see this Sleeping Dragon of a former age.
All the other trees—catalpa, cedar—have rotted away,
leaving only a pair of towering pines.

Poet's note: This year I visited the Shao-pao Pi. Pi's hao [pen name] is Pine Slope. Hsieh's is Pine Screen.

2.

You have seen the ocean turn to red dust,
clouds passing, sand flying—a man of the world!
You are an auspicious treasure of our great dynasty:
who needs magic mushrooms or unicorns?

[The Shao-pao Pi refers to Pi Ch'iang (1517-1608), in his late eighties at the time.]

CLIMBING MOUNT YANG

Craggy rocks, crouching like elephants;
withered pine bark, mottled like fish scales.
From which spot did the Crane Immortal take off?
Is the Dragon Mother possessed of real magic power?
The caves here have talking animals;
on the cliffs live people who never say a word.
The palace of Wu fell apart long ago—
where can the ruins be found?

[See Yüan's prose essay on Mount Yang, translated on pp. 94-95.]

CLIMBING MOUNT HUA

At Shan-sun Pavilion, put on the turban
and become a pilgrim who visits the clouds
          and pays his respects to the rocks.
The waters have a secret method
          for flowing beyond this world;
the mountains are like a drug
          for lightening the body.
Before the eyes, Mount Hua—
          a wall of 10,000 feet.
On the robe—a single speck of dust from the city.
If you come across a chessboard, stay for a while:
before you know it, the wildflowers
          will fade
          and bloom again.

[This poem is one from a group of six. According to legend, a poet once met an immortal near the summit of Mount Hua, and they played a game of *wei-ch'i* chess (Japanese *go*) that lasted through several changes of the seasons. A Pavilion for Playing Chess now stands on this spot.]

AT THE SUMMIT OF MOUNT HUA—
FOR MY FELLOW TRAVELER THE TAOIST SHU

You have walked everywhere on the autumn clouds,
      trod the purple moss,
searched for pine trees on the palm
      of the Great Spirit.
Chang K'ai could conjure up fog
      from his native valley;
Tung-fang Shuo in a former life
      could command the thunder.
You too are a master of Taoist magic,
and you have a sense of humor—
      almost an immortal!
Lotus Peak—a straight drop of 40,000 feet:
only crazy people ever climb this far.

[Chang K'ai of the Latter Han dynasty was said to be able to conjure up fog over an area of five square *li*. Tung-fang Shao was a famous wit of the Former Han dynasty.]

Climbing the Heights on the Double
Ninth Festival at Ho-fu Mountain

High pavilion, overlooking vast cliffs,
and below, stream-paths bordered by flowers.
I imagine that the people who fled
          the government of Ch'in
and entered the mountains
          began their journey here.
Pool waters lap the mountain lichens;
where lichens run out, red mists emerge.
Old dragons clutch skinny rocks;
angry whirlpools, swirling here for a thousand ages.
On the stream, only fishermen;
which of them knows how far the petals float?
No, that story is done, though the white clouds
          are ever new,
and those people are gone,
          though the green mountains remain.
—I hang my bag of dogwood blossoms
          from a branch,
whistle out loud as I lean against a tree
          of cinnabar red.

[The poet alludes to the famous story of Peach Blossom Spring by the poet T'ao
Ch'ien (365-427), which tells of refugees from the cruel Ch'in dynasty who fled
to the mountains and never returned to civilization. It was believed that on the
ninth day of the ninth (lunar) month, the "Double Ninth," one could avert evil
influences by climbing a high mountain with a bag of dogwood blossoms as a
sort of amulet.]

In the Cave of the Jade City

Deep as a valley
high as a hall
penetrating to the heart of clouds
tunneling to the earth's core.
The way is blocked
by stalactites and stalagmites
rocks that look sick
under a crazy sky—
yellow ones of pus
white ones of marrow.
Clouds in floating threads
rise from our boots.
White bats
big as chickens
startled by the torches
flap against our faces.
Suddenly: a peak surges up
then: open and level again.
Dragons want to speak
they hear us and stay quiet
their spittle flows
giving off strange odors.
Ghosts? Immortals?
Mist? Fog?
Our torches give no light
where do we go now?

The ocean can be crossed
the Yangtze traversed
but the Immortal of Spiritual Power
    will be hard to find again.

[See Yüan's prose description of the trip to this cave, translated on p. 96. The Cave of the Jade City is located about ninety *li* from Chu-chi Subprefecture, which is south of Shao-hsing in Chekiang Province. In Taoist lore, caves are frequently seats of spiritual power, or doorways to another magical world. According to a Taoist text of the fourth century A.D., *T'ai-shang ling-pao wu-fu hsü* (Tao tsang, I-wen reprint of 1963, case 22, fascicle 6, pp. 7a ff.), King Ho-lü of Wu once commissioned a semi-divine recluse named Immortal of Dragon-like Power to explore the Lin-wu Cave of Tung-t'ing Mountain. The Immortal (whose name is also given in later texts as "Immortal of Spiritual Power") traveled into the cave for days before returning with a mysterious book. King Ho-lü then sent another messenger to ask Confucius about this volume, and Confucius replied that it was a book of magical charms compiled by the mythical figure Yü the Great. (I am indebted to Nathan Sivin for this reference.) In the present poem, Yüan personifies the mysterious atmosphere of the cave in the figure of the Immortal of Spiritual Power, but also suggests that he himself is like the Immortal in that he too has been exploring a seemingly endless cave.

Yüan's good friend T'ao Wang-ling, who accompanied Yüan on his trip to the cave, has left his own account of the adventure (T'ao Wang-ling, *Hsieh-an chi*, as reprinted by Wei-wen Book and Publishing Co., Ltd., Taipei, 1976, vol. 1, pp. 181-84). Here, T'ao adds some interesting details. He points out that the entrance to the cave was located next to a Buddhist temple, and that some of the monks joined the expedition, bringing along reed mats to help the travelers crawl through the narrow hole, "using the head to lead the buttocks, like a snake." T'ao also points out that the ten or so torches the men carried gave off tiny lights "the size of date stones," so that only the carrier's own body was illuminated, " as if he were an autumn firefly! " The monks of the local temple related the story of an itinerant monk who once traveled further into the cave than anyone, carrying provisions, leaving a trail of chaff, and reciting spells to keep evil spirits at bay. He came upon a great underground stream with a natural stone bridge over it, and then turned back. At the deepest point, the monk was reported to have heard the sounds of boats being rowed way above his head.]

TOGETHER WITH CHU FEI-ERH, WANG I-HSÜ AND TUAN HUI-CHIN I STOPPED AT HSING-CHIAO TEMPLE AND LOOKED OUT AT THE VIEW OF SOUTH MOUNTAIN

The place is ancient—
      no histories say how old;
the terrace, crumbling—
      don't ask when it was built.
Fragrant winds
      blow across Wei Family Ridge;
brilliant snow-light
      sparkles in Fan Stream.
The country temple, half-hidden
      by red maple leaves;
people's houses, interspersed
      with clumps of blue-green lotus.
Across the stream, the mountains
      are still more beautiful—
we mount our horses,
      gallop into the gray mist.

[This poem is one from a group of three.]

Pei-mang Cemetery

Old pine trees, their shaggy manes
      twirled in a dance by the wind;
row on row of tombs, one wisp of smoke
      rising from nowhere.
The lord and princes who once lived
      along Bronze Camel Avenue
have become the dust that settles on the traveler's face.
The white poplar on top of the mountain
      has turned into an old woman
who spends each night in the fields,
      chasing away tigers of stone.
Officials come to this place, face north
      toward the Mausoleum of Longevity,
and give thanks that the crows who perch here
      speak Chinese.

THE CAVE OF THE STONE RAIN

Ask the monks who live on the mountain—
      even they don't know the real name.
The passageways are so narrow
      you must crawl through on your belly.
There are stalagmite clusters, a trickle of stream water,
and other visitors,
      whose voices only
          can be heard.

PAYING MY RESPECTS TO THE MUMMY
OF THE MONK CH'ANG-ERH

The wheel of samsara has come to a peaceful halt;
the gleam of the lacquered body—
      as fresh as a polished mirror!
I know that his soul has long since vanished,
but—amazing!—his nails and teeth are still here.
He is a Buddha of the Age of Adornment,
a human antique, who has lasted a thousand years.
So much for artifacts of bronze or iron—
by now, *they* would have turned to dust!

[For details of the remarkable practice of lacquer-mummification among the
Chinese Buddhists, see Joseph Needham, *Science and Civilization in China*, vol. 5, part
2 (Cambridge, 1974), pp. 299 ff.]

Passing by the Hot Springs
at Hua-ch'ing Palace

Eastern mountains
      and western mountains;
land of Ch'in
      and land of Han.
Light, light clouds
      over the city;
flowing, flowing water
      through past and present.
Crumbling ruins,
      plowed under on terraced slopes;
woodcutters chatting
      as they come home at evening.
Even in decline
      there are "better" and "worse";
King Yu
      was worst of all.

[This poem is one from a group of six. In 723, Hot Spring Palace (Wench'üan kung) was built on Mount Li in Shensi; its name was changed to the Palace of Glorious Purity (Hua-ch'ing kung) in 747. King Yu (r. 781–71 B.C.), the twelfth king of the Chou dynasty, was killed and buried at Mount Li.]

On Hearing That a Girl of the Ts'ui Family
Has Become a Disciple of the Buddhist Master
Wu-nien—Playfully Offered to the Master

She has cut off her conch-shell hairdo,
  thrown away her eyebrow pencil;
the passions have been quenched by a single cup of tea.
Her sandalwood clappers now accompany
  Sanskrit chanting;
her silk dress has been recut:
  a makeshift cassock.
The Master's mind is like quiet water
  reflecting this moon.
His body is a cold forest
  putting forth this blossom.
How many times can she remember
  the hand of ordination
    on her brow?
Generation after generation,
  life after life
    in the family of Buddha!

ROMANTIC SONG

Morning—I come by the avenue of vermilion gateways.
Evening—take my pleasure by bridges over green waters.
The house of songs—get a little drunk and stay ten days.
The dancing girls here—a thousand cash at a time!
This parrot, groggy with sleep, tries to speak;
this dappled horse, swift of foot, gallops without being
          whipped.
I'd rather spend one night with the goddess of Witch
          Mountain
than live on Mount Kou for a thousand years!

[Mount Kou was the site of the apotheosis of Wang Tzu-chin, who took off on
the back of a crane to become an immortal.]

A Woman's Room in Autumn

Autumn colors trickle through the gauze curtains;
cold fragrance floats in, bit by bit.
The chirping of crickets rises from the dark walls;
fireflies flicker in the abandoned loom.
The bedroom fills with new moonlight;
frost on the bamboo screens—
      she changes to warmer clothes.
The migrating goose, the wanderer—
both are gone, only one
      will return.

TWENTY-FIRST DAY OF THE SEVENTH MONTH

A memory returned to me and I wrote this down.

Foggy moon, birdcalls in the flowers at dawn,
in cold willow branches, orioles trembled on the edge of
       dream.
The words "Love Each Other" were written on the pillow,
and heavy incense curled from behind the curtains.

Her emotion had the lucidity of calm waters—
red color came to her cheeks as she smiled!
Back turned to the lamp, she changed her damp nightgown
and asked her lover to gather up her earrings.
Their tears of parting moistened the fragrant quilt,
tenderness of love, fragile as the wings of the cicada!
With silver tongs she stirred the ashes in the brazier
and traced these words: "As Long as the Sky . . ."
Lanterns hung from each story of the building;
the red railing of the balcony gave on the avenue below.

This was the scene of our love that year—
now I see only a tomb, overgrown with grass.
From the roots of the maples, I hear the whispering
       of a ghost
bearing the traces of her southern voice.
The stagnant clouds of this woman's spirit
have been swept into rain
       over a mountain I do not know.

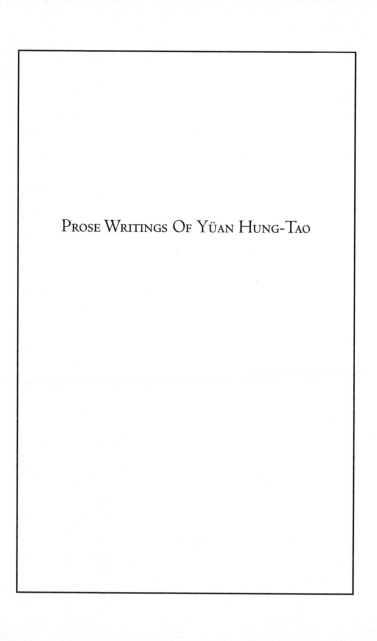

Prose Writings Of Yüan Hung-Tao

Old Jan! Have you written any poems recently? If we don't write poems, how can we make it through these boring days? Human feelings demand some medium of expression—only then can we be happy. So some people do it through chess, some through sex, others through hobbies, and still others through writing. If the wise men of the past were a cut above ordinary people, it was simply because they had means for expressing their feelings; they weren't willing to go floating aimlessly through life.

I often see people who have no way to express their feelings. They run around busily all day long, as if they had lost something. They become depressed for no reason at all; they see beautiful sights and feel no joy. And they themselves can't understand why. This is truly a living hell! Why speak of iron torture racks, bronze pillars, mountains of knife blades, or forests of swords? Oh, what a shame!

All in all, nothing in this world is *that* hard to do—just charge ahead and do it! A day will inevitably come when "the ditch will be dug and the waters flow through." For a man with talent like yours, there is nothing in the world that is impossible. I only fear that you may be overly cautious, that you may be unwilling to take the risk and plunge ahead. Well, force yourself a little! It would be a good idea not to prove yourself undeserving of a friend's encouragement.

Hsiang Sheng-mo (1597–1658): "The Solitary Traveler" (detail). Hanging scroll, ink and colors on paper, 49.5 x 59.7 cm.

Chang Jui-t'u (fl. c. 1624–60: "Illustration to the Second Ode on the Red Cliff of Su Shih" (detail), dated 1628. Handscroll, ink on satin, 320 x 27.9 cm.

Note Written After Chang Yu-yü's Poem
About Hui Mountain Stream

My friend Ch'iu Chang-ju of Ma-ch'eng traveled east to the Wu area, and then traveled back to T'uan-feng with thirty jars of water from Hui Mountain Stream. Chang-ju went ahead by himself, instructing his servants to follow behind with the jars suspended from shoulder-poles. The servants, annoyed by the weight of the water, spilled all of it into the Yangtze. When they reached Tao-kuan River, they refilled the jars with local mountain stream water.

Changju, knowing nothing of this, boasted extravagantly about the water and invited a group of connoisseurs from the city to taste it. When they arrived on schedule, they sat in a circle in Changju's studio with expressions of pleasant anticipation on their faces. A bottle was brought out, as well as porcelain cups, into which just a few drops of the water were poured. These were then passed around for everyone's comments, and then it was time to drink. The connoisseurs savored the water's bouquet for a while, and only then did they sip lightly and swallow, producing a gurgling sound in their throats. They looked at each other, sighed out loud, and said: "What superb water! Were it not for Changju's exquisite taste, how could we ever have had the experience of drinking it in this lifetime!" They went on exclaiming in admiration without pause and then finally left for home.

Half a month later, the servants had an argument in the course of which the facts came out. Chang-ju was outraged and fired the servants involved. As for the connoisseurs who had drunk the water, when they heard about the matter they simply muttered a few embarrassed words.

My younger brother Hsiao-hsiu recently also went on a trip to the east and came back with jars of mountain stream water from Hui Mountain and Chung-leng. He wrote the names of the respective streams on red labels to record which jar came from which stream. When he returned home after a journey of over a month, the writing on the labels had worn off. I asked him: "Which came from Hui Mountain and which from Chung-leng?" He couldn't tell. And even after drinking some water from each jar, he still couldn't tell. We looked at each other and roared with laughter.

But in actual fact, Hui Mountain water is far superior to water from Chung-leng, let alone Tao-kuan River! Since coming to the Wu area myself as magistrate, I have tasted the waters many times and I am now able to distinguish among them. Reading the present poem by Yu-yü reminded me of these things that happened in the past, and before I knew it, I was doubled over with laughter! This affair was similar to the "appreciation of pork at Ho-yang" of which Su Tung-p'o wrote, so I have written about it to provide Yu-yü with a good laugh.

[Chang Yu-yü probably refers to Chang Hsien-i, an authority on the *I Ching* (Book of Changes). Ch'iu Chang-ju was Yüan's friend, Ch'iu T'an, and Hsiao-hsiu was Yüan's younger brother, Yüan Chung-tao.]

A Record of the Hall of Bhaishajyaguru, the Medicine Buddha

At the Monastery of Pure Compassion, Master Lien's compound is the most remote. The pathway leading to it twists and turns for perhaps a bit over a third of a mile from the temple gate. Lining the path are many old trees and various kinds of plants. The compound fronts on Lotus Flower Villa and has Dharma Flower Terrace behind it.

My younger brother Hsiao-hsiu once stayed at this place while discussing Ch'an Buddhism with Chiang Lan-chü, and this year I stayed here during every one of the three trips I took to West Lake to see the flowers with T'ao Shih-k'uei and Fang Tzu-kung. When I come here, I am never in the least displeased, nor am I in the least uncomfortable. When I have to leave, I always hesitate, held back by lingering affection for the place.

Why is this? Other monasteries are filled with pilgrims, tourists, and women devotees, coming and going and generally making a racket, as if the place were a public courtyard. master Lien closes his door and has nothing to do with worldly affairs. This is one delightful thing about this place.

Monks who are obsessed with purity often force people to eat a vegetarian diet. I cannot stand such a diet and Master Lien does not force one upon me, nor does he become angry when my servant smells up the pots, jars, bottles, and dishes by cooking meat. This is a second delightful thing.

Paying my respects to Master Lien's friends, the brothers Yü Chang-ju and Seng-ju, is a third delightful thing.

Master Lien comprehends the Buddhist dharma, but does not put on the airs of a priest. he can write poetry, but does not put on the airs of a poet. This is a fourth delightful thing.

My younger brother is extremely coarse and loud, yet Master Lien does not resent him. As for me, I am wild and strange by nature and I write many crazy poems. I am arrogant and highly emotional and do not keep the various Buddhas in mind. But for all this, Master Lien does not consider me foolish. This is a fifth delightful thing.

Now, one person's likes may not coincide with someone else's. The things Master Lien approves of are not necessarily the things that please me. But the Master hardly ever expresses disapproval. Being pleased with the place, I stay here. Staying here, I enjoy myself, Enjoying myself, I feel comfortable, Feeling comfortable, I hesitate to leave, with lingering affection. All this makes perfect sense. What I do feel somewhat ashamed of is that although I am an official, I cannot requisition one dollar, and when I am a traveler, I cannot *find* one dollar. While I am a donor of the temple in name, I cannot come up with half a cent to donate! Perhaps I could say a word or two on behalf of the temple to those of my friends who are in office, but those who are living in retirement are forced to be stingy and cannot do much to help. What sort of person must the Tathagata Bhaishajyaguru of Radiant Light think I am?

Nevertheless, if I should in a future life become a

Buddha of Abundant Jewels, I will make a donation to this temple of as many pieces of gold as there are particles of sand in the Ganges River so as to fulfill my present vow. I have no desire to become any other sort of Buddha.

According to Master Lien's records, this place used to be called Pure Residence Hut, but now forms part of the temple complex. There is one hall in which an image of the Medicine Buddha is enshrined—this image was completed in the fifth month of the year *ting-yu* [1597]. Behind the hall is a storied building where the monks perform the recitation of Buddha's name. There are two side-cloisters along which the monks' cells are located. Downstairs in the storied building, facing south and to the right, is a small, clean room that I have made use of for a long time.

Because Master Lien happened to ask for a record of this spot, I have written away freely, putting down whatever came to mind. Each phrase may seem like a joke, but the words are all accurate. When future scholars read this essay, will they be angry or will they smile?

[Master Lien (or Lien-ch'ih) was Chu-hung (1535-1615), a major figure in Ming-dynasty Buddhism (see Introduction). T'ao Shih-k'uei and Fang Tzu-kung were the author's friends T'ao Wang-ling (1562-1609) and Fang Wen-tsun (d. 1609). The Yü brothers were Yü Ch'un-hsi (tzu, or style name, Chang-ju, d. 1621) and his younger brother Ch'un-chen (tzu Sengju). T'ao, Fang, and the Yü brothers were all followers of Chu-hung, as were the Yüan brothers.]

Sitting at night in Pure Temple, I talked with my friend Fang and our conversation turned to the subject of strange dreams.

Fang said: "I once had a dream that was extremely bizarre. I came upon a district office with vermilion gateway and guards holding elaborate halberds, as if it were a king's palace. I entered by way of the eastern staircase and noticed that in front of the main hall were two high towers with a ferocious looking guard standing in each. These two men had red hair and green eyes—they were terrifying in appearance. On the central dais were standing three giants, several tens of feet tall, their bodies covered with strings of jewels. When I asked someone who they were, he answered: 'These are the demigods.' Next, I approached the dais, and one of the giants asked: 'Do you wish to observe your former life?' Beside me was a man in a black robe, who immediately led me out of the hall to the eastern corridor. There I saw a monk sitting on a reed mat, holding a wooden fish gong. His face was haggard and jaundiced, and his expression was one of depression and dissatisfaction.

"When I had finished looking at him, I was led back to the main hall, where the giant again questioned me: 'Do you wish to observe your next life?' Before he had finished speaking, a guard leaped down from one of the towers and brandished the iron cudgel he was holding above his head. Sparks flashed from it in all directions, and the giants and buildings all disappeared. Then the guard led me to a little hole, out of which he dragged a man whose neck was in fetters, whose hair was burned, and whose clothes were filthy. This, I realized, was myself. And so I began trying to imagine what evil deeds I had performed in my present life to merit such suffering, and then, weeping, I awoke."

Fang also said: "Once, when my late mother was still alive, I dreamed of a demon orderly who was holding a tally, similar to the ones used by attendants in our provincial and district offices. On it was inscribed my mother's name. It happened that a nephew on my sister's side was also present, and the two of us wept and pleaded with the demon: 'We desire to reduce our own allotted years to prolong mother's life!' The demon pointed to my nephew and said: 'How could a distaff relative be allowed to do this?' Jumping with excitement, I exclaimed: 'If that's so, you can subtract ten years from my life!' The demon orderly nodded yes and left. Exactly ten years later, my mother died."

With this, I said to Fang: "Your physiognomy is not that of a long-lived man, and your life span has been reduced by ten years. How many years could you have left? The time when you'll be wearing those fetters is drawing near!"

For a long time after this, Fang looked quite unhappy.

[Fang was Fang Wen-tsun (d. 1609).]

I sat at night in Shuang-ch'ing Villa, trading recent ghost stories with T'ao Shih-k'uei.

Shih-k'uei said: "Last year my sister-in-law died. On the day of her death, one of our maidservants suddenly went crazy, saying that she was the wife of X from N village, that she had died of strangulation and had followed her fellow ghosts to this place to beg for food, and that as they were leaving, her way had been blocked by the masses of ghosts; she could not advance and so had been left behind. Now she was famished and pleaded for a single grain of rice. As she beseeched us to give her food, her manner was pitiful and moving in the extreme. After a while, some cooked rice was brought. The girl fell flat on the ground and snapped out of it as if waking from sleep. When we questioned her, she could not remember a thing."

T'ao also said: "In my home district, in the family of a certain scholar-official, the wife became ill. Suddenly she exclaimed that the girl X, or the young lady X, or the uncle X, or the nephew X had arrived. All of these were people who had been dead for one, two, or even ten years, and yet one was able to converse with them as if with living persons. After several days, the woman suddenly said that Yama had come to beat her. Immediately, she fell to the ground, writhing beneath the blows of the stick. Her screams of pain could be heard near and far, and all over her body there appeared welts, as if produced by a stick. Then she kneeled on the ground, motioning with her hands as if to ward off the stick—her ten fingers turned black and blue and started to drip blood. Next she began twisting and turning on her bed as quick as the wind. When someone questioned her, she said: 'Yama is grinding me!' The manifestations of her suffering were a hundred times more horrible than anything in ordinary life. After a few more days she recovered enough to claim that she had originally been an immortal in heaven who had been banished to this earth. She had forgotten her old life and had behaved enviously and jealously in this one, so she had been punished while still alive. Now that the punishment was over, she could return to heaven. When she had finished speaking, she died."

T'ao said further: "Recently, one of my cousin's grandsons, who had been married for less than six months, was visited night after night by a certain beautiful woman who would sleep with him. Eventually she became his concubine. Before long, her actions became extremely strange, and she kept telling people that in this world there was nothing desirable, other than death—nothing else could bring her happiness. Several times she attempted to hang herself with her stocking laces or to throw herself into the water. Her people would stand around and keep watch over her, but one night the person who was guarding her dozed off, and the woman killed herself by jumping down the toilet. This is quite similar to the affair of Li the Red."

These stories are all worth recording, so I have written them down here to expand the available accounts of strange matters.

[T'ao Shih-k'uei was T'ao Wanq-ling (1562-1609). Li the Red, a T'ang dynasty poet who gave himself this name because he felt his poems were comparable to those of Li Po (" Li the White"), is said to have died by falling into a toilet, after which he was accorded the dubious distinction of being called the Toilet Demon. Yama is King of Hell in both Indian and Chinese tradition. For a good summary of modern anthropological interpretations of female possession, see I. M. Lewis, *Ecstatic Religion* (London, 1971).]

RECORDING SOMETHING WEIRD

When I went to Ch'i-yün, I heard there was a Taoist who claimed that he knew of a wealthy ghost. I asked him about this and he said: "In N district, the woman X died in pregnancy and was buried at a certain spot. Every evening thereafter, she would appear in the marketplace, hugging a child to her breast and begging for food. Someone recognized her and exclaimed: 'That's the wife of X! She's been dead for half a year!' When the husband was told of this, he had the coffin exhumed and discovered that lying next to the dead woman was a baby boy breathing very faintly. The father took him out and raised him. Now the boy is over forty and has amassed a fortune of ten thousand cash."

I asked some people from Anhui Province about the matter, and they all said: "This happened quite recently— you can ask the man himself to come and talk with you, if you want."

This is very close to a story in the book *Pien-ching kou-i*, so we can see that the weird events of past and present are often similar. How can one discuss everything under the sky with Confucian pedants?

My friend Fang said: "I have heard the monks of Cloud Perch Temple assert that if one recites Buddha's name, one may achieve birth in the Pure Land. Is this true?"

I replied: "Yes. Without going into all the written accounts, let me just refer to cases I have experienced myself. Tung, the second son of my elder brother Po-hsiu, became terminally ill at the age of twelve. He himself knew he had no hope of living. When he was on the point of dying, he spoke to me tearfully: 'I will die today. Is there any way to save me?' I answered: 'If you only recite Buddha's name, you will immediately be reborn in Buddha's land. The present world, with its Five Ages of Decay, is not worth yearning for. Just concentrate on Buddha with one mind and all will be well.'

"I then had my nephew chant Buddha's name while holding the palms of his hands together in an attitude of devotion. The entire family stood around him in a circle, praising Buddha in rich tones. After a while, my nephew smiled slightly and said: 'I see a lotus flower, the color of earth, but slightly reddish.' He then continued to chant. After some more time, he suddenly spoke of the extreme brilliance of the lotus, which he said was incomparably superior to any in this world, and was now bigger than before. Still another period of time—and suddenly, he said that Buddha had arrived, the radiance of his features filling the entire room! A little later he said that there was an impure person in the room, whose presence had caused the lotus and Buddha to disappear. Po-hsiu looked around and noticed that a maidservant, who had just arrived, was standing in front of the folding screen. This girl, as it happened, had just had her period that evening, so Po-hsiu called to her to leave and had the other people encircle his son and chant Buddha's name as before. The boy then grew short of breath, and Po-hsiu said: 'If you just recite one character of my name, that will be enough.' The boy asked me: 'Is that all right?' and I replied: 'Yes.' But when he had chanted a few syllables more, he died, still holding his palms together.

"My second maternal aunt-through-marriage, the lady Chu, heard of our discussions of Buddhist matters and was herself a believer in the recitation of Buddha's name. Some time ago, I got a letter from Hsiao-hsiu, in which he wrote: 'Three days before our aunt died, she called all her sons before her and said that Buddha had announced he would come to greet her within three days. At the appointed time, she took a bath and sat in the main hall, surrounded by her family, waiting. After a long time, she said: "Buddha is here!" and passed away.'

"These two cases come from my own personal experience and are therefore most reliable."

Fang laughed and said: "If this is true, then those fetters of mine can be thrown off on the spot!"

[Fang refers to Fang Wen-tsun. Po-hsiu and Hsino-hsiu were Yüan's elder brother, Tsung-tao, and younger brother, Chung-tao. According to the second chapter of the Lotus Sutra, Buddha said: " The Buddhas appear in the evil ages of the five decays, that is to say, decay of the kalpa, decay through tribulations, decay of all living creatures, decay of views, and decay of lifetime." (As translated by Bunno Kato, with revisions by W. E. Soothill, Wilhelm Schiffer, and Yoshiro Tamura, *The Threefold Lotus Sutra*, New York and Tokyo, 1975, p. 61.) For "Those fetters of mine . . ." see Yüan's essay "Dreams," translated on pp. 92-93.]

Raising Crickets

In the capital, people in every family keep crickets as pets during the seventh and eighth months. I go out to the fields beyond the city, where I see old men and young boys—crowds of them—in the grass, ears cocked and walking back and forth with serious expressions on their faces, as if they had lost something important. As soon as they hear the slightest chirp, even if it comes from some dirty wall or filthy outhouse, they run over and pounce on their prey like a famished cat that has spotted a mouse! Holding their clay pots and jars, all the people of the entire city do the same. And then, old and young, male and female—every citizen brings his cricket out to fight with others, just for fun.

There is a variety of cricket, something like a locust but plumper, that the people of the capital call "Blabbermouth," and which they also catch and keep as a pet. Southerners call this type "Weaving Lady." It eats the flowers and the pulp of the sponge gourd plant and sounds something like the common cricket, but is superior in clarity and intensity of tone.

I once had two of them in cages, which I hung from the eaves. Their piercing chirps penetrated the night, mournful, extraordinary—purifying my ears. Reading as a youth at the Tu family estate, drying my hair in the pine-tree forest...these scenes and images were brought back to me as clearly as if they were right before my eyes. No sound, whether the croaking of bullfrogs or the crying of cranes, could possible compare.

Another variety is also something like the common cricket, and when its tones ring out, they seem to have been produced by metal gongs or jade chimes. The sound is rich and resonant, and creates a feeling of peace in those who hear it. The people of the capital call this type the "Golden Bell." When it sees darkness, it chirps; as soon as light returns, it stops. Neither this nor the previous variety can fight, so they are not as popular as the common cricket.

I once read a book by Chia Ch'iu called the *Classic of Crickets.* In sum, the book says that these insects that are born among earth and grasss are weak of body, while those born among tiles and stones will be strong of body. Those born in places where foliage is sparse and the soil thin or where tiles and stones block access to the sunlight, will be mean of spirit. Also, white crickets are inferior to black ones. Black ones are inferior to red ones. Red ones are inferior to yellow ones. Yellow ones are inferior to green ones. The best of all are the "white hemp heads" with green necks, gold wings, and gold and silver streaking on their foreheads. Next come the "yellow hemp heads." And finally, those of gold-purple-

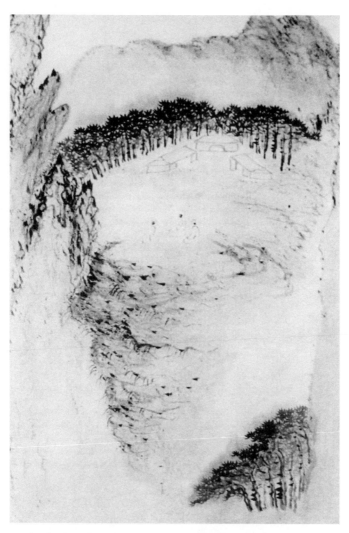

Attributed to Mei Ch'ing (1623–97): "Scene in the Yellow Mountain" (detail).
Hanging scroll, ink and colors on paper, 105.4 x 40.6 cm.

Wen Po-jen (1502–c. 1575): "Dwellings of the Immortals Amid Streams and Mountains" (detail). Hanging scroll, ink and colors on paper, 177.8 x 62.9 cm.

black hues. In terms of form, the best have thick heads and necks, long legs, and broad-backed bodies. Inferior to these are crickets with narrow heads and necks, skinny legs, and meager thighs.

The insects suffer from four types of illness: "upright head," "drooping antennae," "stumble-foot," and "worn jaws." Should the cricket contract any of these, he will be useless.

Names for crickets include: White Tooth, Green Puller, Yellow Belly, Red Head, Purple Dog, Yellow Rope, Embroidered Raincoat, Living Hoe, Golden Orient Sash, Straight Backbone Wings, Plum Blossom Wings, Crow-head Gold Wings, Oiled-paper Lamp, Three-piece Embroidery, Red Bell Moon, Fragrant Forehead, and Mottled Shoulder Bell. And there are a great many others like these, too numerous to list in full.

As for feeding crickets, use *kuei* perch, the fleshy part of water chestnuts, "reed-root" insects, "broken-joint" insects and "shoulder-pole" insects. These should be thoroughly boiled with chestnuts and coarse rice.

The cricket can be kept healthy as follows: for worn jaws, feed it mosquitoes that have some blood in them; for fever, use the pointed leaves of bean sprouts; for excretory disorders, use female shrimp; for dizziness, bathe it with tea made from the *ch'iung* herb of Szechwan; for bite wounds, daub the injured area with a mixture of boy's urine and worm droppings.

Thus *The Classic* details every conceivable aspect of the

forms and habits of crickets. Indeed, if such are the subtleties and complexities of a single insect, it is possible to conclude that the circumstances of even lice or gnats are not that different from those of human beings.

[The character that appears in the text for the second word in the phrase "Mottled Shoulder Bell" is not to be found in the dictionaries. It is assumed that it is a nonstandard variant for *chien*, "shoulder." In the sentence beginning "As for feeding crickets . . . ," the translator has not been able to identify the last three items; the translation of the entire passage remains tentative.]

ANT FIGHTS

Once as I was passing through West Mountain, I saw some boys take several large ants out of a pine tree, cut off their antennae, and make them fight and bite each other to the death. When I asked about this, the boys said: "Ants use their antennae as eyes. Whenever they want to move, they first explore to the left and the right with their antennae, and only then do they move quickly ahead. As soon as the antennae are cut off, the ants are unable to walk; they become angry at not being able to see and will fight to the death because of this." I have tried it out for myself and found it to be true.

It seems to me that the idea of ants seeing with their antennae was never mentioned by the ancients. Also ants do have eyes, so it is particularly remarkable that they should depend upon their antennae for forward movement. I have therefore recorded this matter for future scholars of living creatures.

SPIDER FIGHTS

The technique of making spiders fight each other, as far as I know, has never been mentioned in the past. My friend Kung San-mu invented this sport. When we were young, San-mu and I were roommates. Often, in gentle spring weather, we would look for little spiders with longish legs, each of us capturing several; then we would keep them on our window sill and enjoy ourselves by making them fight.

Spiders often can be found in the dark places of walls or under tables or desks. Their webs may consist of only a few strands, warp without woof. When catching them, one should not act nervously, or else they will be frightened; once frightened, a spider will not be able to fight for the rest of its life. The female ones are preferable to the male, which run away when confronted with an opponent. The male's feet are somewhat shorter and the belly thinner, so it is easy to tell the difference.

The method of training them is as follows; first take the unhatched eggs of another spider and place them on the paper portion of a window. When the female spider sees the eggs, she will think that they are her own children and will protect them with passion. If she sees another spider approaching, she will think it has come to attack and will fight it with all her strength. Spiders that are carrying eggs themselves or have produced eggs before should not be used.

At this time of battle, the spiders first strike each other with their legs. After several such passes, they become more and more ferocious, and their angry claws fly so fast that one cannot even see their bodies! The winner ties up the loser with webbing, only stopping when the opponent has finally died. Sometimes, however, one spider will become weak with fright and will retreat in mid-battle, and there are also cases when the two are so evenly matched that they both give up after several passes. San-mu is always able to guess in advance which will win and which will lose, and even at the moment of catching them, he can say immediately; "This one is a good fighter; this one is not. This one and this one are perfectly equal." Later, it always turns out to be as he predicted.

The best spiders are dark; gray ones are second best, and mottled ones are inferior.

And there are many names for spiders, such as Black Tiger, Eagle Claws, Tortoise-shell Belly, Black Chang Ching, Yaksha Head, Happy Lady, and Little Iron Mouth. All of these names are based on the spiders' forms.

San-mu feeds the spiders flies and big ants. He knows exactly how to tell when they are hungry or satisfied, happy or angry. In fact, there are too many details to record fully here.

San-mu is a man of brilliance, and a poet as well. He can master any art or pastime known in the world after the slightest acquaintance with it. But it is true that he has neglected his studies as a result.

[There are several men with the name Chang Ching in Chinese history, including an animal and bird painter who was praised by Mi Fu(1051-1107), and a military official (chin-shih degree 1517) famous for his campaign against Japanese pirates.]

A rich man who had suffered disappointment in a certain matter came to live at Ti Mountain for a while. He bowed to a recluse of that place and said: "To be as poor and ill as you are, sir, is something which anyone would hate, and yet your manner is as pleasant as the springtime, and your expression as clear as the moon after the rain clouds have disappeared. How strange!"

The recluse said: "There's nothing strange about it! Some time ago I vomited up blood and could not get out of bed for an entire year after that. The best doctors were unable to help me. I was sure that I would die and, in fact, it was rumored that I had already died. There was nothing I could do about it—I heard people speaking of my own death and, to my amazement, I got better! From this point of view, my present life is unexpected, and whatever comes to me in this life must be counted as unexpected gain. It is simple human nature that when one experiences unexpected gain, one cannot feel unhappy even if one tries."

The rich man said: "You live in obscurity here in the mountains What could possibly happen to you that you would count as gain and feel happy about? This is stranger still!"

I said: "There's nothing strange about it! I keep in mind that in the recent past my two feet wouldn't hold me up, and now I can walk about—this is happiness! My arms could hardly move, and now I can paddle a boat—this is happiness!

My waist and back could not support my weight, and now I can bend or lean as I please—this is happiness! Nor was I ever comfortable when lying down, and now I sleep soundly with peaceful snores—this is happiness! So, if you consider most people's desires and satisfactions to be happiness, then my unhappiness would be ten thousand times greater than yours. But if you consider my walking, standing, sitting, and lying down to be happiness, then you ought to be ten thousand times happier than me! What's so strange about that!"

The rich man said: "Nevertheless, you were ill and on the brink of death. It is for this reason that you developed your present views. As for me, I have never been ill and never on the brink of death."

I said: "Since I am able to maintain the point of view of a man on the brink of death, even though I am actually not on the brink of death, why should you not be able to cultivate the point of view of a seriously ill man even though you are not ill?"

With this, the rich man finally realized what I was saying and, relaxing his expression and laughing out loud, he said: "Amazing! You are able to be happy and to make me happy too! Amazing!"

I said: "There's nothing amazing about it. The other day, I was walking below the city wall with a friend. We saw a beggar coming toward us, pleading mournfully. This beggar had a small head and face, delicate skin, a refined voice, and was walking slowly, as if each step was difficult. I assumed that this was a woman beggar, so I asked: 'Do you have a husband?' The beggar smiled faintly. I thought that perhaps the beggar did not understand the word 'husband,' so I asked: 'Do you have an old man?' The beggar smiled once again, as if slightly embarrassed. I said to my friend: 'Can it be that when romantic matters are brought up, even a beggar will be pleased?' At which the beggar said with a smile: 'I'm a man!' My friend and I realized that we had been wrong all along, so we laughed out loud, and the beggar laughed too."

I said: "You have come from far away—there are people who give you gruel, some who give you rice, and some who even give you money. In none of these cases do you forget that you are a beggar, so you never laugh. Now, just a moment ago when you laughed, did you feel that you were a beggar? When you forget that you are a beggar, you no longer are a beggar—you are the same as anyone else, the same as a rich man, the same as a nobleman with a fief of ten thousand households! Have I not given you something wonderful?'

"The beggar agreed, thanked me with a smile, and left.

"Now, if I can make a beggar happy, shouldn't I be able to make a rich man like yourself happy? There's nothing amazing here!"

Such was the profundity of our conversation that the rich man forgot to leave. Mist encircled the darkening mountains; a temple bell sounded from the distant trees. I had already lent the man the use of my sleeping platform; now I tossed him the thick mat I had been sitting on as well.

He laughed and said: "I have heard that there are people who weep at night because they have no roofs over their heads. How could they ever get to stay in a warm house, with such a fine mat to sleep on?" Then he fell asleep.

[When the speaker switches to the first person it becomes clear that the recluse is Yüan himself.]

TIGER HILL

Tiger Hill is perhaps seven or eight *li* outside the city walls [of Suchou]. The hill itself is lacking in precipitous cliffs or deep ravines, but simply because of its proximity to the city, not a day goes by without flutes, drums, and fancy boats clustering there. On any moonlit night, flowery morning, or snowy evening, visitors come and go like the threads of some great tapestry, and the day of the Midautumn Festival is the most popular time of all.

Every year, when this day comes around, the entire city empties out and every citizen goes to Tiger Hill, walking shoulder to shoulder with the rest of the crowd. From the families of high officials down to the people from the slums, everyone dresses up in his or her best clothes, the women put on their finest make-up, and they all bring along reed mats to sit on and wine to drink as they walk down the roads.

From Thousand Man Rock all the way up to the gateway to the mountain, the people are packed together like the teeth of a comb or scales on a fish. There are so many musical clapping blocks being played that one could pile them up into a mountain of their own. Wine flows like rain from clouds. If you look at the whole scene from a distance, it is as if a flock of wild geese were landing on a beach or clouds were spreading out above the Yangtze River; claps of thunder, flashes of lightning—really, there is no way to describe it!

When the mats are laid in place, over a thousand singers perform, producing a sound like swarming mosquitoes—it is impossible to distinguish any one singer's voice! But then they are divided into teams, which compete in a singing contest. Once the refined have been separated from the vulgar, and the beautiful from the ugly, it is no time at all before there are only several tens of performers still swaying their heads and stamping their feet. By now, the moon has floated up in the sky, making the rocks look like radiant silk. All the "earthen crocks" have been silenced, and only three or four musicians are still playing. One transverse flute, one short flute, and one person beating the clappers slowly and singing —wind instruments and voice in perfect harmony, clear, penetrating sound . . . all who hear are swept away! Then, at midnight—moon shadows slanting everywhere, water plants bending every which way—the flutes and clappers are laid aside, and a man appears on stage. The audience nearly stops breathing. The man sings—the tone is as fine as a thin hair, yet carries far beyond the clouds. He takes fifteen minutes to complete the melisma on a single word! The passing birds linger to hear him, strong men weep at the sound.

As for the nearby sights, Sword Spring is deep beyond fathoming, surrounded by soaring cliffs which seem to have been hacked out of the rock. The "thousand acres of cloud," with the mountains around the Pool of Heaven as their resting place—peaks and gullies vying in beauty—create a perfect spot for entertaining guests. The only problem is that after twelve noon the sunlight shines directly in and one cannot sit there for too long.

The Pavilion Where Literature Flourishes is also fine. The evening trees here are particularly worth seeing. If you look to the north from this place, you will see the ruins of P'ingyüan Hall and a vast, limitless view beyond, the only discernible feature being the peak of Mount Yü. This hall was abandoned long ago. Chiang Chin-chih and I once discussed ways to restore it, hoping to enshrine such poets as Wei Ying-wu [736-c. 792] and Po Chü-i [772-846] therein, but I became ill and petitioned for release from my duties, and I am afraid Chin-chih also lost interest in the project. Is it possible that the fate of beautiful places also depends on the vicissitudes of time?

I was magistrate of Wu for two years, and during that period I climbed Tiger Hill on six occasions. The last of these was when Chiang Chin-chih, Fang Tzu-kung, and I went together. A late moon rose above the public terrace, and when the singers heard that the magistrate had come, they all disappeared! I said to Chin-chih: "How terrible, the cruelty of officials and the vulgarity of clerks! On some future date, when I have left office, if I do not come back to hear the singing on this terrace, may the moon take me to task!"

Today I have, fortunately, been able to retire, and I can indeed be called a "traveler in Wu!" I wonder if the moon at Tiger Hill still remembers my words?

[The use of the phrase "earthen crocks," which originally suggested the triumph of the vulgar in government, derives from a poem of the third century B.C. in the Ch'u tz'u anthology, *Pu chü*. David Hawkes, *Ch'u Tz'u: The Songs of the South* (Oxford, 1959), p. 89, translates the relevant passage as follows: "The brazen bell is smashed and discarded; the earthen crock is thunderously sounded. / The slanderer proudly struts; the wise man lurks unknown." The character for the last word in the phrase "as fine as a thin hair" does not appear in the *K'ang-hsi Dictionary*. It is assumed that this character is based upon a cursive variant of *fa*, "hair." Anyone who has had an opportunity to hear the brilliant English countertenor Alfred Deller will understand what is being described here: a high, seemingly thin voice that is nevertheless extremely resonant and has an almost uncanny ability to carry great distances. The "thousand acres of cloud" is apparently the name of some kind of pavilion. Chiang Ying-k'o (Chin-chih) lived from 1556 to 1605. For a useful description of some of the sights mentioned in this essay see Marc F. Wilson and Kwan S. Wong, *Friends of Wen Cheng-ming* (New York, 1975), pp. 12-14.]

Mount Yang surges above all the surrounding mountains and connects with a range which extends over a distance of several tens of *li*. It falls under the jurisdiction of two subprefectures. Beneath the mountain is the Shrine of the White Dragon. According to the old people of the area, during the Eastern Chin dynasty (317-419), an elderly man wearing a white robe once stayed overnight at the house of a commoner and left the next day. The woman of the house became pregnant and later gave birth to a white dragon, complete with horns on its head. This dragon rose up into the sky and the woman was frightened to death.

Now, beneath the mountain, there is the Tomb of the Dragon's Mother, with a cypress tree in front of it that is some twenty spans in circumference. Several years ago, a white dragon was seen hanging from one of its branches like a bolt of silk, swaying back and forth and looking around as if trying to find its parents. Whenever there is a drought and the people here pray for rain, they are sure to be answered. Because of the magic power of the spot, it has been recorded in the official annals of ritual.

This year, in the sixth month, the drought demon acted up again, and Chiang Chin-chih and I accompanied the prefect when he prayed for rain at the shrine. As he started, intense sunlight was glittering in the pool and not a sliver of cloud was to be seen anywhere in the sky. Chin-chih and I climbed to the summit, and just as we reached Arrow Tower, on all four sides clouds and fog arose from the mountains, forming a vast, gray mass in which one could not distinguish anything. Then, in the time it takes to inhale and exhale, rain poured clown in torrents, filling the rice paddies with water. Chin-chih and I looked at each other in terror and left as quickly as we could.

Is it possible that dragons really are divine creatures?

[Mount Yang is located northwest of Wu-hsien, near Great Lake (T'ai-hu) in Chiangsu Province. See Yüan's poem on Mount Yang, translated on p. 69.]

The Jade City is over twenty *li* from the Five Waterfalls. The entrance to the cave is broad and the interior is at first like a huge mansion. After one has gone in a way, the path narrows slightly, then returns to its former breadth. Within the cave, rocks in the shapes of lotus flowers or human figures are numerous. There are three or four turnings, and then a hole that is so narrow that one can only get through by crawling. The two T'ao brothers and I went through flat on our bellies, lighting our way with torches. Smoke filled the available space, so that our tears fell like rain. Then I remembered hearing an old story about people suffocating because of torch smoke in caves; I became frightened and retreated, along with the T'aos. Only Wang Ching-hsu and an office clerk of Wu Subprefecture went ahead at the risk of their lives. They crossed four or five ridges, coming to the innermost depths of the cave, found their way blocked by a subterranean stream, and only then turned back.

[See Yüan's poem on this cave, translated on p. 73.]

Hundred Flowers embankment is located between the Hsü and P'an city gates. One evening, I strolled out through the P'an gate and happened to meet Chiang Chin-chih on the road. he said: "I wonder if the flowers at Hundred Flowers Embankment are in full bloom yet? Why don't we go take a look?" I said: "The only thing you'll find there is a string of twenty or thirty barges filled with night soil, moored one after the other like tightly packed scales on a fish and stinking up the air for miles."

Chih-chih laughed out loud, and we parted.

Solitary Mountain

The recluse of Solitary Mountain had "a plum tree as his wife and cranes as his children." This was the highest man of leisure in the world! Such people as myself and my friends, precisely because we have wives and children, let ourselves in for all kinds of problems. We cannot get rid of them, and yet we are tired of being with them—it's like wearing a coat with tattered cotton padding and walking through a field of brambles and stickers that tug at your clothes with each step!

Recently, a man named Yü Seng-ju has taken up residence beneath Thunder Peak, and he too has no wife. Perhaps he is a reincarnation of the recluse of Solitary Mountain! He has written a group of poems on plum blossoms falling in the creek, and while I do not know how they might be felt to compare with the poetry of the recluse, he did turn out 150 of them in one night, which can certainly be called writing quickly! As for his practice of fasting and doing Zen meditation, this actually puts him a cut above the recluse.

Is there ever an age without remarkable men?

"The recluse of Solitary Mountain" was Lin Pu (967–1028), a major poet of the early Sung dynasty. Yü Sen-ju also figures in Yüan's essay "A Record of the Hall of Bhaishajyaguru . . . ," translated on pp. 89–91.

Of all the mountains around West Lake, Flew-Here must be considered the best. While it is no more than a few hundred feet high, it stands like a huge chunk of blue-green jade. One could not do justice to its angry posture, even by calling it a thirsty tiger or a galloping lion. One could not do justice to its strange form, even by speaking of gods weeping and demons rising. One could not do justice to its colors, even by referring to autumn floods or evening mist. Nor could one do justice to its twisting, turning transformations, even by comparing it with the calligraphy of Crazy Chang or the painting of Wu Tao-tzu.

The many weird trees that grow on the mountain's rocks do not depend on soil—their roots jut out above the stone! There are four or five caves in all, large ones and small ones, which let through a mysterious light, and in which liquid drips into stalactites. The shapes seem to have been cut or carved. The Buddha images sculpted into the rock were in fact created by Baldhead Yang, but these, like scars on the face of a beautiful woman, are unfortunate, ugly flaws.

Altogether, I have climbed Flew-Here Peak five times. The first time, I made the trip with Huang Tao-yüan and Fang Tzu-kung. We wore unlined shirts rolled up in back, and we made it right to the summit, known as Lotus Flower Point. Each time we came upon an unusual rock, we would without fail go wild with excitement and let out loud shouts. The next time, I climbed with Wang Wen-hsi, then with T'ao

Shihk'uei and Chou Hai-ning, then with Wang Ching-hsu, T'ao Shih-k'uei, and Shih-k'uei's younger brother, and finally with Lu Hsiu-ning. Every time I made the trip, I thought of writing a poem, but I have never been able to write one.

[Flew-Here Peak (Fei-lai feng), near Hangchou, is dotted with caves whose walls are ornamented with Buddhist relief sculptures. Many of these were carved under the supervision of a Tibetan or Mongolian monk named Yang-lien-chen-chia (Baldhead Yang) around 1300, and show Lamaist influence. The monk was hated for his desecration of the tombs of the Southern Sung emperors. For a discussion of the carvings in English, see Heather Karmay, *Early Sino-Tibetan Art* (Warminister, England, 1975), p. 24. For illustrations, see Huang Yung-ch'üan, *Hang-chou Yüan-tai-shih-k'u i-shu* [The Art of the Yüan Dynasty Stone Caves at Hangchou] (Peking, 1958).]

...I once expressed the thought that West Lake is like a painting by one of the Sung-dynasty masters, and the scenery at Shan-yin is like a painting by one of the Yüan dynasty masters. Flowers, birds, and human figures, all visible in every detail, rich and sparse areas, distant and near scenes, every color exquisitely fine: such is the scenery of West Lake. People without discernible features, trees without discernible branches, mountains without discernible vegetation, water without discernible ripples, everything abbreviated or suggested, the sense of distance arising from the forms; such is the scenery of Shan-yin. As to the question of which of the two is superior, I leave that to people possessed of a perceptive eye.

Shin-yin became famous in the Six Dynasties period, and became less popular starting with the T'ang. West Lake became known in the T'ang and is at its peak of popularity now. Perhaps scenic spots also undergo the vicissitudes of fate!

A Record of Listening to the Rock of Echoing Waters

The rock is halfway up Heaven's Eye Mountain. If you listen to it quietly, the sound of flowing water can be heard from within, resonant and clear. Its name is The Rock of Echoing Waters. This rock is over twenty feet high, and twice this in breadth. It is strangely beautiful in its outer form and powerfully structured beneath the surface.

Let this serve to remedy the omission of this rock from rock catalogues of the past.

[Heaven's Eye Mountain is located east of T'ai-hsien in Chiangsu Province.]

The Heavenly Gate of the mountain called Even-with-the-Clouds is a beautiful spot, but unfortunately the area below the cliff is cluttered up with inscriptions and epigraphs. How irritating! The people of Anhui just love to write graffiti; this is a shortcoming of theirs. And the officials who have held office there have been influenced by local custom. Even the small rocks are all covered with vermilion characters or plain engraved words. It's enough to make one gasp with anger!

I have noted that the law provides for standard punishments for those who plunder the mountains or dig illegal mine shafts. Why is it that vulgar scholar-officials can desecrate the Mountain Spirit with impunity? Buddhism says that all evil action will lead to appropriate retribution. The acts I am describing are in a class with murder and robbery, and yet Buddhism makes no mention of them. This is an oversight on the part of the canon.

What crime have the green mountains and white rocks ever committed, that their face should be branded and their skin cut? Oh, how inhumane!

The rocks at the Peaks of the Five Elders are all beautiful but slightly lacking in rich luster. Also, the mountain forms themselves are not that spectacular, so visitors need not stay too long. If the Taoist shrines would reduce the number of their rooms, then officials would come here less frequently. Eventually, the inscriptions would become effaced, lichens would cover the rock, and, unless the god of this mountain is totally lacking in spiritual efficacy, in less than one hundred or so years, Even-with-the-Clouds should return to its pristine beauty.

My fellow travelers were Mei Chi-pao, T'ao chou-wang, P'an Ching-shen, Fang Tzu-kung, the monk Pi-hui, and the two gentlemen Chang and Li. We stayed for five nights, then continued traveling.

[For the phrase "rocks at the Peaks of the Five Elders . . ," an alternative version of the text has been partially followed.]

A Record of Staying Overnight
at the Terrace of Falling Stones

After coming down from Even-with-the-Clouds, we took a raft downstream to the Terrace of Falling Stones. Here, stones have fallen along the bank of the stream, creating a cliff on top of which one could spread out a mat. The monks living on shore were not friendly, and when they heard that some travelers had arrived, they closed the doors to their chambers.

The building closest to the nearby mountain was very picturesque, so I said to Shih-k'uei: "Let's just barge in! Who needs to ask the monks?" I dragged Shih-k'uei in with me, and the others followed timidly. The sunlight glittering on the stream and the blue-green colors of the mountain seemed to reflect off the tables and benches.

Two youths then appeared and bowed to us. They had expressions of serenity on their faces. Indicating Shih-k'uei, one of our group said; "This is the venerable T'ao of K'uai-chi." The youths immediately jumped to attention, bowed, and went to set out some wine for us in the pavilion. We discussed the life of an examination candidate with them until midnight. The sound of the stream penetrated the night like the wind in ten thousand pines.

The next morning, the youths asked us for poems and plaque inscriptions. I named the pavilion "Stream Sound." Shih-k'uei said: "This is the rain I dreamed of at Heaven's Eye!" So I named the studio "Dreaming of Rain." We each wrote two poems for the occasion and gave them to the youths.

A RECORD OF A TRIP TO CH'UNG-KUO TEMPLE

It was the year *chi-hai* [1599], the third day of the third month. It had been decided that Po-hsiu, Chao-su, Sheng-po, and myself would celebrate the customary day of purification beside the river beyond the west gate of the city, but because a sandstorm started up, we took shelter in Ch'ung-kuo

Temple.

As it happened, Wang Chang-fu and my younger brother were having a literary gathering at this very place, so we all got drunk together and had smiles on our faces the whole day. Everyone agreed that this was our first real intoxication since the beginning of spring.

One of the temple monks then led us to see the image of Tutor Yao. Yao was dignified and imposing, and his eyes seemed to flash like lightning. The inscription consisted of the words: "My true nature is that of a monk," written out by the Tutor in his own calligraphy.

Next, we visited the hostel for foreign monks, and here we saw images of Manjushri and other figures. One had a blue face and the head of a boar; it was fat and dwarfish, wore human heads all over its body, had sixteen legs arranged in parallel fashion, and held many kinds of weapons. This image was extremely ferocious in appearance. The monk explained that it had been presented by the Tibetans, who brought many images of this kind, and he also told us about the customs of Tibet and how far away it was. In sum, it can be said that the provinces of Tibet consider even the lowest grade of Chinese tea to be a national treasure and use it as a medium of exchange. Gold and silver, strangely enough, are not in circulation. The country is without rice paddies, and the people eat only wheat and pulse. There is a local overlord for every several tens of *li*, something like the administrative system of China. But is is a backward, impoverished country.

At this point, Po-hsiu and Chao-su left because they had

official duties to attend to the following morning. The rest of us talked about the *I Ching* [Book of Changes] until midnight. New points of discussion kept coming up as we talked, and we did not want to leave but, as our servants had been waiting a long time in the cold night, we had no choice but to go.

[Tutor Yao was Yao Kunag-hsiao (1335–1418), who became a monk at the age of fourteen, but resumed a lay name when appointed Tutor to the Heir Apparent. He was a poet and a painter, as well as one of the most influential political advisers of his day. For further commentary on this essay, see the Appendix.]

A RECORD OF TRAVELING
FROM CLOUD PEAK TEMPLE TO HEAVENLY POOL TEMPLE

Above Cloud Peak Temple, the way becomes more and more precipitous. Green cliffs and deep valleys twist and turn as one walks. What is it that sticks to one's sandals like clumps of cotton—clouds! What is it that gives off the mysterious sounds of strings brushed by the wind! Where is it that a single rock forms a bridge, one thin path a hundred feet long spanning a drip of hundreds of yards?—Silken Creek Bridge. Where is it that clumped reds and entwined greens coil and spiral as they lead one's way—the Mountain of the

Ninefold Screen, also called the Mountain of Nine Banners. Which mountain looks angry and determined, like a ferocious warrior standing alone and intimidating everyone?— Iron Boat Peak.

Every several *li*, we stopped for a rest, and five times came upon places where the vegetation at the top of a cliff had been cleared away to make room for a pavilion. The path was steep and dangerous, and we had to use hiking sticks a we climbed. Each time we came to a stream, we would roll up leaves to use as drinking cups.

After passing Shih-hsin Rock, we had a view of Bamboo Grove Temple from the rear. The sound of a spring and the wind in the trees created the effect of Sanskrit chanting. At this point, there were no more pilgrimage pavilions. Instead, a group of temple structures jutted up into the sky, surrounded by peaks like screens. It was as if we were halfway to the empyrean! The Buddha halls were highly ornate and had metal roofs. A stream swollen with green waters, flowed musically at the bottom of the stairs.

When we had rested a bit, we climbed to the Terrace of Manjushri. Looking down, we saw the back of a circling hawk. And farther below, a thousand acres seemed small enough to fit in a cup. A moment later, curling clouds began to emerge from below the rocks. They floated around the pines and continued on, like smoke from brewing tea rising to the trees. Then these clouds took on the forms of human figures, birds, and animals, and suddenly the ground was completely covered by them. Everywhere we looked, great waves seemed to surge and flow. We held on to the pine trees as we sat on the rock—above us was blue sky and below, white clouds! This was the ultimate in mysterious transformation.

Later, we went to tell the monks what we had seen, but they said: "It's always like that here—nothing to talk about!"

[The places mentioned in this essay all form part of Mount Lu in Chianghsi Province. Mount Lu was one of China's most famous mountains, and was visited and written about by a number of great poets.]

Excerpt from a Diary

. . . We took boats down the I River to visit the Caves of the Thousand Buddhas at Lung-men. Many of the caves on the western bank were carved in the Wei period [386–554], and the Buddha images have an archaic simplicity about them. Dedicatory inscriptions are engraved right into the rock, written in the calligraphy of the northern dynasties [386–581]. Unfortunately, these are badly effaced. The caves of the eastern bank are fewer in number, but the faces and drapery folds are depicted in an extremely free manner, so that the images are full of life and seem on the verge of breaking into speech! In one cave are engraved sutra texts, in a style reminiscent of Ch'u Ho-nan. There is also a stele inscribed with the writing of Emperor Shen-tsung [r. 1068–85] of the Sung dynasty, in excellent condition but half buried in the ground. The names on the walls are mostly those of people from the K'ai-yüan [713–41] and Ta-li [766–79] eras.

Evening fell and we were forced to leave without having seen everything.

The Buddhist caves at Lung-men are well known and have been frequently written about: e.g., Peter C. Swann et al., *Chinese Monumental Art* (New York, 1963), pp. 102 ff. Ch'u Ho-nan was Ch'u Sui-liang (596–658), one of the great calligraphers of the T'ang dynasty.

On a certain day, I went to the Office of Tribute Inspections, where I met an envoy from Annam. The tribute he had brought consisted of gold and silver vessels, which were embellished with rather unskillful designs. Aside from this, he had only brought a little sandalwood, laka-wood, and ivory.

I asked this envoy whether he could do calligraphy, and he said: "I can." So I gave him a brush, and he wrote out a quatrain in cursive script [*ts'ao-shu*]:

> The path meanders over a stone bridge,
> > the stream bends nine times;
> the clouds veil an embankment of bamboo groves
> > with three little houses.
> The gates are half closed,
> > wildflowers are falling;
> one cry from a bird—a calm day in spring.

His cursive was virtually impossible to read, so I asked him to write the standard forms beside each character, and these were no different from the ones used here in China.

[The Annamese (Vietnamese), like the Koreans and Japanese, wrote much of their poetry in Chinese, partly because they admired Chinese culture and wished to emulate it, and partly because this ability proved useful in dealing with Chinese diplomats and officials.]

A Biography of the Old Drunkard

The Old Drunkard—no one knows where he comes from. Nor has he told anyone his name. Since he's always drunk, I call him the Old Drunkard. Each year he travels between north and south China. He wears a seven-brim hat and embroidered robes; he has high cheekbones and a broad jawbone. His beard hangs down to his belly—to look at him, you'd think he was a ferocious general. He is perhaps fifty years old or so, but has no companions or followers. In his hand he carries a yellow bamboo basket. He spends the entire day dead drunk and seems asleep even in broad daylight. The stench of his boozy breath can be smelled a hundred paces away. He walks the streets looking for wine and, in a short while, he has drunk at over ten wine shops!—yet he seems no drunker than before.

The Old Drunkard does not eat a grain diet; he eats only centipedes, spiders, toads, and any sort of insect. The children in town are terrified of him—they grab whatever vermin they can find and offer these to him to eat. Wherever he walks, over one hundred people can always be seen trailing after him and staring. If anyone insults him, he rattles off a few words, some of which inevitably touch upon an intimate secret of that person, who then runs away in fright.

In his basket, the Old Drunkard always carries several tens of dried centipedes. If asked why, he says: "When it's cold, you can still get wine, but you can't get any of these."

When Po-hsiu told me about this man, I thought the

whole thing was an exaggeration, so I invited him to my house for a drink. The boy servant found more than ten verminous insects and offered them to him. He swallowed all of them alive! Each little bug he would dip in his wine cup, as one dips chicken in vinegar, and then he would wash them down with wine. As for the centipedes, which were five or six inches long, he would pick up each one with cedar needles, remove their pincers, then place them, still alive, in his mouth. The red legs could be seen moving frantically between his whiskered lips: all of us got goose flesh just watching! But the Old Drunkard was obviously enjoying himself, chewing away with relish, as if he were dining upon essence of bear or suckling pig. When he was asked which delicacies were his favorite, he replied: "Scorpions taste wonderful, but unfortunately you can't get them down south. Centipedes are second best, and of the spiders, I prefer small ones. But you shouldn't eat too many ants, because they'll make you depressed." Then I asked what benefit he derived from his diet, and he said: "None! I do it just for fun!"

After this, the Old Drunkard and I became quite close. Whenever he came, he would crouch down on the stairs, call for wine, and drink away. If anyone treated him like an honored guest, he would immediately show his displeasure. He talked on and on about many strange subjects. Every so often, something he said would be truly mysterious, but he he would not answer any inquiries about it, and if I repeatedly questioned him, he would purposely change the subject.

One day I went out with my uncles, and we were speaking about the beautiful sights at Gold Mountain and Mount Chiao, when we met the Old Drunkard along the road. My second uncle mentioned that in a certain year he had climbed Gold Mountain. The Old Drunkard smiled and said: "Could it be that the military adviser so-and-so was host, and the secretary so-and-so also went along? My uncle was astonished, but when the Old Drunkard was asked how he had come to know these things, he did not answer. At a later time, someone managed to take a quick look into his basket and saw something like a certificate of official appointment in it. He claimed that the Old Drunkard had been a well-endowed official in the area, which seemed to make sense.

The Old Drunkard's behavior was truly bizarre. He had no fixed home. At night he would stay at an old shrine or beneath the eaves of the city gates. He was constantly repeating the words: "All dharmas return to the One—where does the One return?" whether moving about, staying in one place, sitting, sleeping, or conversing. If anyone asked him why, he would not answer.

Once when I was on my way to an official post, I saw him again at Sha-shih, but I do not know where he is now.

Shih-kung says: I often see strange people in the cities and regret that I know nothing about their lives. And I regret that of the strange people holed up in the forests and mountains, probably only one out of ten appears in the cities! As for the strange people recorded in the official records and unofficial books, surely they represent no more than one-tenth of those who do appear in the cities. Since these are people with no ambition to become known, and since they associate only with butchers, wine merchants, shop owners, wandering monks, and beggars, how many worthy scholar-officials even get to know about them and hand down their stories? In the past, I have heard of a woman known as the Cap-wearing Immortal, and a Taoist of the Single Gourd, both living in Feng-chou. Recently, several people in the Wu-han area have been acting quite strange, and one of them seems to know a thing or two about the Tao. Yes, it appears that this is what is meant by the old saying: "Though he possesses the powers of a dragon, he remains hidden."

Shih-kung was one of Yüan's names. An account of the eccentric Taoist of the Single Gourd by Yüan Chung-tao is translated on pp. 155-157. "Though he possesses . . . " is a quotation from the "Wen-yen," one of the appendices to the *I Ching*. This passage occurs in the commentary to the first line of the first hexagram, *ch'ien*.

POEMS BY YÜAN TSUNG-TAO

CENSOR LIU HAS BEEN LIVING IN EXILE FOR SEVERAL
MONTHS; HE HAS SENT ME A JAR OF WINE THAT HAS KEPT
ME DEAD DRUNK FOR DAYS

Liu has been away quite some time now.
From his distant exile, he sends a jar of wine!
The jar is huge—holds five gallons;
the carrier's shoulders must be aching with pain!
The wine is fresher than water from Hui Spring,
whiter than milk from Snow Mountain.
And it makes me remember what happened last year:
the debate at court, the depositions . . .
then the Censor submitted his memorial to the throne
with a trace of criticism in its wording.
He was banished to the provincial office of Liao-yang,
a demotion in rank, but a gain in fame.
He got this wine on credit—his salary ran out—
and sent the fine brew to an old friend.
Now I don't have boring breakfasts anymore;
every morning I pour from the jar and drink.
I'm in a daze, it's all like a dream . . .
sunning myself under the eaves, I open a book,
rub my eyes and read each word out loud
until slanting sunlight strikes the snow on the stairs
glittering like golden particles of sand.

The Studio of Ten Thousand Gibbons

What is there in your studio?
A lute and some books, companions
      to your solitary bed,
and the sound of reading out loud,
which mingles with the cries of the gibbons.

Wine

Fine wine! I pour it into a cup of rhinoceros horn
and it gives off the faint fragrance of evergreens.
To help it down, celery and parsley;
I feel as if I'm living in the mountains!
There's no need to cook any pork or lamb;
this is subtle wine, and doesn't go with greasy meat.
My cheeks have been red for three days now,
but I have spent fewer than a hundred coins from my purse.
So I don't waste a thing, and I'm no glutton either.
I care for my livelihood and my stomach as well!
Those who hold office here in the capital
only enjoy these two things:
Number One—lots of good wine.
Number Two—plenty of friends.
So here's how to keep from getting homesick:
call your friends over and get drunk now and then!

Eating Fish and Bamboo Shoots

Bamboo shoots—the salt of the earth!
Fish from the river—no money spent!
Just let me eat this way for the rest of my years;
everyone is welcome to get ahead of me in life.

Relations with people? In retirement
      I've come to understand.
My heart of ice? Grown tougher
      with the years.
Rain-streaked window, green branches
      slanting outside:
a good place to get drunk,
      a good place to sleep.

Watching Clouds in the Mountains

The clouds look like piled-up mountains.
The mountains look like gathering clouds.
Clouds, mountains—how do you tell the difference?—
The clouds are white, the mountains are green.

Things Seen on the Road to Hsin-Yang

1.

Sheer cliffs surround the rice paddies.
A little path lets through carriage and horse.
This, this is Peach Blossom Spring;
why keep trying to find the way?

2.

I look all around me—no road at all!
Driver, where are we going?
Suddenly I hear the whinny of a horse
that seems to come from empty sky.

3.

Below the mountain, no signs of people.
On the mountain, no bird calls.
This leaves only the single wisp of cloud
to watch me ride through this place.

4.

From the clouds, unexpected, barking and crowing!
Could it be the home of the immortal Liu An?
Looking more closely—blue smoke from kitchens!
There is a village ahead on a mountain ridge.

5.

The driver looks back, frightened:
"There's a tiger howling in the woods!"
But no, at the foot of the cliff
a mountain torrent roars against the rock.

6.

Beyond the bridge, mountains piled high.
Along the bridge, rocks like bristling teeth.
They serve to gladden the traveler's heart,
but also to hurt the horses' feet.

THE MONK SSU-HSIN DECIDED ONE MORNING TO LEAVE HIS LIFE AS A DEGREE CANDIDATE, TOOK THE TONSURE, AND BECAME A MONK; I HAVE WRITTEN THESE POEMS TO SEND TO HIM

I.

Do you want to know who the new monk is?
He used to be Yüan Chung-fu!
He has the same old holes in his head;
only a few whiskers are missing.

2.

Your boastful spirit
        and the hairs on your head—
one sweeping cut
        and they all fell away!
There is only your love for the mountains:
that, no razor can trim.

[These are two poems from a group of six.]

FOR THREE DAYS I TRAVELED THROUGH MOUNTAINS;
WHEN THE MOUNTAINS CAME TO AN END
I WAS DEEPLY MOVED

Before my eyes, green mountains—
       I have truly loved them.
Why not have their craggy heights before me every day?
But this morning, the curtain fell,
       the mountains were swept away,
and I felt unhappy, as if I were saying goodbye
       to a friend.

CROSSING THE YELLOW RIVER

Our carriage races beneath newly cleared skies.
Crisp air rises from green peaks.
On and on . . . until we see the vast river,
the vast river that flows endlessly.
The official in charge of the docks tells us
last night's rains have swollen the river.
In a tiny boat, we set out across huge spaces;
surging waves splash over the side.
Oars straining, we move out on the river;
we cannot tell which way is east or west.
Then—thunder is heard, rumbling of chariots,
and clouds like snow-covered houses jostle each other.
My children's faces turn the color of ashes,
but as for me, I feel like a king!
"This ship of state I entrust to the loyal Minister Kuan!
No fear that my wife, Lady Ts'ai, will rock the boat!"
The boatman seems possessed—
he hoists the sail, and we come to no harm.
But what power does a boatman have?
For protection, we depend on the bounty of the gods.
The one-inch heart of this pedantic bookworm:
Thank you, River God, for sparing it!
I mutter reassuring words to my children—
"You have nothing to be frightened about!
There are many windy waves in the ocean of bureaucracy,
and they are much worse than the waves of the Yellow River!"

["This ship of state . . . rock the boat!": The poet briefly imagines himself to be Duke Huan of Ch'i, who in the seventh century B.C. achieved hegemony over the other feudal lords of China by following the advice of his brilliant minister, Kuan Chung. The episode of Lady Ts'ai is recounted in the *Tso chuan*, a historical chronicle of the third century B.C., and also involves Duke Huan of Ch'i: "The marquis of T'se [Duke Huan of Ch'i] and Ke of Ts'ae [Lady Ts'ai] were in a boat on a lake in the park, when she made it rock. The marquis was afraid, changed colour, and forbade her; but she persisted. The marquis was angry, and sent her back to Ts'ae, without absolutely putting her away [i.e., without divorcing her formally; she was his wife]. They married her away there, however, to another." Duke Huan was later to take revenge by attacking the state of Ts'ai. (Translation from James Legge, *The Chinese Classics*, vol. 5, p. 138; interpolations by J. C.)]

POEMS AND PROSE BY YUAN CHUNG-TAO

A Yüan-Dynasty Painting of
a Lohan at Ta-te Temple

We take it out of the box,
          feel it with our hands,
                    recognize Yüan-dynasty silk;
the drapery folds are like water
          rippling as it flows.
Long ears, long eyebrows,
          eyes that glitter at you—
if you look from close up, nothing is clear,
          look from further back!
On the dark surface—no inscription can be found
and the monks do not know the date.
But there is a tradition
          handed down from the founder of the temple
that says this is a self-portrait
          by a supernatural monk
                    from the West.

A Wild Crane

A wild crane stands in the field of rice sprouts.
He sees someone and flies up in fear,
flies low for twenty or thirty feet,
then, as before, settles back onto the field.

KEEPING A PET ROOSTER

I have a friend in the capital
who has made me a gift of a pet rooster.
He has sharp spurs, a high comb,
and colorful markings—a fine appearance!
He beats his wings and crows out loud,
flies over the walls and into my room.
He sheds feathers on the bookcase
and leaves scratches all over my zither.
My servant says: "Kill it!
Kill it and eat it for supper!"
Suddenly I hear the sound of a knife being sharpened;
tears come to my eyes, and I sigh:
"I can do without the taste of fowl,
but it's a matter of life and death for him!"
I throw down my book, run into the kitchen,
and hold back my servant, with scolding and curses.
The rooster is still terrified:
he cowers in a dark corner of the room.
Chirping, chirping—the bird in the cage
wants to fly away, and has wings.
Glistening, glistening—the fish in the net
plunges back in the water as soon as there's a chance.
I want to let the rooster go
but he'll never escape the butcher's knife.
The best thing to do is to keep him
and let him stay always on his favorite perch.

Don't say it's another mouth to feed—
a few kernels of grain in a bowl—
      how much is that to spare?

WALKING ALONG THE WILLOW EMBANKMENT OUTSIDE THE WEST GATE

After Po-hsi's death

As in the past
    graceful willows
        cover the long bank
and the sun sinks
    west, west
        of the thousand trees.
There is only the sound
    of the river
        which is different than before:
then it sounded like laughter to me,
    now it sounds like weeping.

[Po-hsiu was the poet's eldest brother.]

MISCELLANEOUS POEM AT THREE LAKES

Distant water
      spread out behind misty trees
with a few black dots
      among the waves:
it is like a newly finished painting,
the rich ink still slightly moist.

[One poem from a group of seven.]

SNOW AT THE RIVER PAVILION OF WANG LUNG-HSÜ

1.

The little building rests on rock,
roof tiles splashed by spray from the waves.
Traveler, don't lean against the railing:
that's the Yangtze River down below!

2.

Biting cold—I stop arranging my books.
My face is still flushed from the morning wine.
I lean on the table, but can't fall asleep,
listening to the battle between water and rock.

3.

Brilliant white, covering the whole bank,
and along the bank, a thousand masts.
I see no one in the boats,
only snow, on the boats.

4.

The guests here—really happy.
The water and rocks—really mad.
At sunset, no boats on the river,
only a pair of white egrets.

5.

Stick out your hand—a handful of river water!
Use it to wash the inkstone.
But move that wine jar away from the window:
the passing sailboats may knock it down.

6.

The river is white in itself;
now brilliant snow fills sky and earth.
The river has a sound of its own;
now add the roar of a furious wind.

Drinking in the Mountains

Heavy rain clouds rise before our wine cups,
dense rains start to fall.
Let's sprinkle some wine into the clouds—
the people on earth below
      will catch the smell of wine.

Mourning for the Scholar
Huang Shen-hsüan

The northern tower
      is where we spoke from our hearts.
The western hill
      is where we wept at parting.
I have always admired your actions—
      understated, like those of the ancients—
and I remember your compassionate face.
No more Green Plum Calligraphies
      will come from your hand
and the red strings of your zither
      are broken forever.
Where is your soul wandering now?
Come to me in dream
      and let me know.

[This poem is one of a group of ten. Huang Shen-hsüan was Huang Hui (1554-1612), poet and friend of the Yüan brothers. The Green Plum Calligraphy was a famous masterpiece by the calligrapher Wang Hsi-chih (307-65).]

POEM OF EMOTION

In a mountain village among the pine trees
I want to build a tower of three stories.
The highest story would be a place of tranquility
where I would burn incense and practice meditation.
The middle story would be for my books;
here, the wind would blow softly from the pine trees.
In my right hand I would hold the sutra of Vimalakirti,
in my left, the works of Master Chuang Tzu.
The bottom story would hold my singing girls;
here, I would give parties and invite people to enjoy
          themselves.
From the four corners would float fragrant perfumes,
from the center would rise beautiful songs.
          The guests are already intoxicated from listening
                    to the music,
          they try to leave but I have thrown their linchpins
                    away!
          In the room is one young singing girl
          whose name is Never Grieve.
          She can dance the Dance of the Seven Turns
          and sing a hundred tunes with her jewel-like voice.
          On ordinary days I have no visitors
          but, full of pride, take the place of honor myself.
          Today, let us enjoy the greatest pleasure of all:
          please, take out your zither and play for me!

[This is one poem from a group of fifty-eight.]

A Biography of the Taoist of the Single Gourd

The Taoist of the Single Gourd—no one knows his real name. He used to wander about in the O and Yüeh region [i.e., Hupei] carrying only a single gourd, so people dubbed him the Taoist of the Single Gourd. Since the Taoist passed away in Feng-chou, the people of Feng-chou have come to be familiar with the facts of his life. They have told me the following:

The Taoist when young studied books, but feeling dissatisfied with this, he gave up his studies, went to the seacoast, and became a soldier. At that time the Japanese pirates were at their height. In the battle against them, the Taoist was an unusually brave fighter, and rose to the rank of major and ultimately to that of colonel. Later, however, he broke the law and, fearful of being punished, took refuge with a band of robbers. With them he knocked about the Ch'u region for a while, but eventually he tired of this life as well. His next move was to purchase on credit over ten singing girls and become a restaurateur in the Huai River-Yangchou area. Whatever profits he took in he kept entirely for his personal use, and the singing girls did double duty by waiting on him at all times. Not a day went by when he was not surrounded by beautiful women, with meat to eat and wine to drink, and music played on string and wind instruments to listen to. The food, drink, and service he enjoyed were comparable to those of any proper gentleman. But again, after ten or so years of this, he became bored, gave it all up, and became a beggar in the region of Lake Tung-t'ing.

Finally, he came to Feng-chou. At first, the people of Feng-chou did not know who he was, but after a while he made a few wild statements that turned out to be strangely prophetic. He also gave out various medicines that were always effective, painted pictures of water buffaloes, improvised poems on the spot with some remarkable phrases in them, and before long people came to respect him. They made him gifts of food and clothing, all of which he would accept and then throw away. But this only inspired the people to entertain him even more lavishly.

The Taoist lived in an old shrine. One day he took an ingot of gold out of the brazier, gave it to the shrine intendant, and said: "Do me a favor and hire a monk to come here and say the last rites." When the rites were finished, he bought a coffin, removed the cover, sat inside, and had ten or so men carry him through the streets while he held his hands in the posture of reverence and shouted: "For years I've been a great burden to all of you—now I would like to say good-bye! "Even in the tiniest alleys people crowded around to see him. The whole city was amazed. At last he returned to the shrine, lay back in the coffin, and said to the crowd: "Now you can cover me! "No one dared obey this command, but when they looked into the coffin they found that he had already died! So they put the cover on and buried him. When the coffin was lifted, it was found to be extremely light, as if there were no corpse inside.

When I heard about this I was quite fascinated. A friend

had this to say: "When we consider men of the Tao, we find that it is inappropriate for them to be lascivious or for them to commit burglary. Those who are lascivious or who commit burglary cannot be expected to transcend life and death. I am greatly puzzled." When he put this problem to me, I replied: "You and I are mere mortals. How can we expect to understand this? Think of Crazy Chi's love for wine, Three Wagons's love for meat, Linked Bones's promiscuity, the vile language of Han Shan and Shih Te. Only a man possessed of heavenly vision can comprehend these things. Among the Buddhas of ancient times, there were those who disguised themselves in the forms of pigs and dogs. How much less unlikely would this be in this be in the case of a human form? Can you or I possibly hope to understand this!"

[Crazy Chi was Tao-chi, a famous Buddhist monk of the Sung, dynasty known for his love of wine and meat. Three Wragons was the T'ang-dynasty monk K'uei-chi, a disciple of Hsüan-tsang. He needed three wagons to carry all his posses-sions; hence his nickname. Linked Bones was probably the nickname of another Buddhist monk. Bodhisattvas were said to have linked bones. Han Shan and Shih Te were the semi-legendary Buddhist eccentrics of the T'ang dynasty.]

APPENDIX:

A NOTE ON SINO-TIBETAN RELATIONS
AND YÜAN HUNG-TAO'S DESCRIPTION OF A TIBETAN SCULPTURE

The essay "A Record of a Trip to Ch'ung-kuo Temple" contains what must be one of the earliest detailed descriptions of a Tibetan work of art by a Chinese writer. According to David Snellgrove and Hugh Richardson in their book *A Cultural History of Tibet* (New York and Washington, 1968, p. 156), ". . . there was no fixed relationship . . . between the rulers of Tibet and the emperors of the Ming dynasty, but contact was maintained by the frequent visits to China of monks and lamas of the great Tibetan monasteries.... Chinese diplomatic fictions describe these as 'tribute missions.'" The same writers point out that Chinese painting was beginning to influence Tibetan art early in the Ming dynasty, and Yüan's essay serves as a reminder that Tibetan monks were reciprocating by bringing examples of their native art to China. We know that in the Wan-li era (1573–1619) Tibetan envoys were presenting "painted Buddhas, bronze Buddhas," and other items to China as "tribute"; these facts are recorded in the dynastic history of the Ming dynasty! (as quoted in Giuseppe Tucci, *Tibetan Painted Scrolls*, Rome, 1949, vol. 2, pp. 693–94)

The image described by Yüan Hung-tao, which could be either a painting or a painted statue (probably one of the small bronzes for which Tibetan art is famous), was probably a representation of Yamalitaka, the most horrific form of the Bodhisattva of wisdom, Manjushri. Yamantaka, whose function was to subdue Yama, the King of Death, had in turn several manifestations, the most extreme of which, Vajrabhairava, is described in the iconographical texts as having nine heads (the main one of which was that of a bull), thirty-four arms, and sixteen legs. He is black and naked, wears a long, meandering belt of human heads, and holds a chopper, a sword, a skull, a drum, etc. (Antoinette K. Gordon, *The Iconography of Tibetan Lamaism*, revised edition, Rutland and Tokyo, 1959, p. 88 and p. 91). If we consider that the bull's head of Yamantaka might easily have been confused with that of a boar by a non-Tibetan, and that the black of the painted statues is often closer to a dark blue, Yüan's account of the image he saw could be entirely accurate. Particularly significant is his reference to the parallel arrangement of the legs; on every image of Yamantaka, the left legs, which are straight, are perfectly parallel to each other while the right legs, which are bent, are also perfectly parallel. (For an excellent example of a painted bronze Yamantaka, dating from the seventeenth century, see F. Sierksma, *Tibet's Terrifying Deities*, Rutland and Tokyo, 1966, plate 1.)

It is also of interest to note that as early as the Yung-lo era (1403–24) Tibetan-style bronzes were being made in China, probably by Tibetan craftsmen employed in imperial workshops (Heather Karmay, *Early Sino-Tibetan Art*, Warminster, England, 1975, p. 97), and that Yarnantaka was in their repertoire (Karmay, fig. 62 on p. 91). It should be kept in mind, however, that the image described by Yuan was actually brought to China from Tibet.

Robert Van Gulik, in his book *Sexual Life in Ancient China* (Leiden, 1961, pp. 259–61; cited by Heather Karmay, Early Sino-Tibetan Art, p. 100, n. 14), calls attention to two passages in which Lamaist statues are described (it is not clear whether these were Tibetan imports or Sino-Tibetan products made in China): Cheng Ssu-hsiao (1239–1316) in his Hsin-shih and T'ien I-heng (fl. c. 1570) in his Liu-ch'ing jih-cha. But the incredible rituals described by Cheng (including human sacrifice, vampirism, and cannibalism, to name only a few), and his blatantly anti-Lamaist stance must call into question the accuracy of the entire passage, while T'ien I-heng's essay also is polemical in nature. Yuan Hung-tao is simply intrigued by the image itself and describes it in more detail than is found in either Cheng Ssu-hsiao or T'ien I-heng. He does not moralize.

Also, Van Gulik's implication that Cheng describes a Yamantaka image is misleading: Cheng does not specifically refer to this iconographical type (see *Hsin-shih*, Peking, 1939 edition, pp. 129–30). Thus Yüan's essay testifies both to his considerable powers of observation and to his ability to transcend ethnocentrism and express interest in the achievements of another culture.

Finally, Snellgrove and Richardson (PP. 158–59) also inform us that tea was introduced into Tibet from China probably as early as the eighth century. The Tibetans, who brewed their tea with butter and salt, came to regard it as a favorite beverage. In addition, Snellgrove and Richardson report that "to offer tea-ceremonies on a vast scale to a community of monks became a recognized act of merit."

I have used the edition of Yüan Hung-tao's writings published by the *Shih-chieh shu chü*, Taipei, 1964: *Yüan Chung-lang ch'üan chi.* This consists of the following five sections, each with independent pagination:

1. *Yüan Chung-lang wen-ch'ao* (abbreviated here as WC)
2. *Yüan Chung-lang shih-chi* (SC)
3. *Yüan Chung-lang ch'ih-tu* (CT)
4. *Yüan Chung-lang sui-pi* (SP)
5. *Yüan Chung-lang yu-chi* (YC)

The Wei-Wen Book and Publishing Co., Ltd, of Taipei has issued a reprint in four volumes of a Ming edition of Yüan's writings, first published in 1629 (1976; from a copy in the National Central Library, Taipei).

Iriya Yoshitaka En Kodo [Yüan Hung-tao], *Chugoku shijin senshu*, series 2, vol. 11, Tokyo, 1963 (abbreviated here as Iriya), is an anthology of poems by Yüan with introduction, Japanese translations, and commentaries.

Yang Te-pen, *Yüan Chung-lang chih wen-hsüeh ssu-hsiang* [the Literary Thought of Yüan Hung-tao], Taipei, 1976, is a recent Chinese-language study of Yüan.

The most thorough discussion of Yüan in English is a University of Wisconsin (Madison) Ph.D. dissertation by Hung Ming-shui; "Yüan Hung-tao and the Late Ming Literary and Intellectual Movement" (1974), D.A.I. Order No., 75–9978.

For Yüan Tsung-tao, I have used *Yüan Po-hsiu ch'üan chi, Basic Sinological Series*, Shanghai, 1936; and for Yüan Chung-tao, *K'o-hsüeh chai shih-chi* and *wen-chi*, Shanghai, 1936.

Some poetry of the period will be found in Wu-chi Liu and Irving Yucheng Lo, ed., *Sunflower Splendor*, Bloomington, 1975. A series of anthologies of poetry of the later dynasties being prepared by Irving Lo should add considerably to the few available English translations of this material. For the philosophical and religious background of the period, see William Theodore deBary, ed., *Self and Society in Ming Thought*, New York and London, 1970; and William Theodore deBary and the Conference on Seventeenth-Century Chinese Thought, *The Unfolding of Neo-Confucianism*, New York and London, 1975.

For the painting of the period, see James Cahill, *The Restless Landscape: Chinese Painting of the Late Ming Period*, University Art Museum, Berkeley, 1971.

COMPANIONS FOR THE JOURNEY SERIES

This series presents inspirational work by well-known writers
in a small-book format designed to be carried along
on your journey through life.

Volume 9
Pilgrim of the Clouds
Poems and Essays from Ming China
Translated by Jonathan Chaves
1-893996-39-5   5 x 7   164 pages $15.00

Volume 8
The Unswept Path
Contemporary American Haiku
Edited by John Brandi and Dennis Maloney
1-893996-38-7   5 X 7   224 pages $15.00

Volume 7
Lotus Moon
The Poetry of Rengetsu
Translated by John Stevens
Afterword by Bonnie Myotai Treace
1-893996-36-0   5 x 7   132 pages $14.00

Volume 6
A Zen Forest: Zen Sayings
Translated by Soioku Shigematsu
Preface by Gary Snyder
1-893996-30-1   5 x 7   140 pages $14.00

Volume 5
Back Roads to Far Towns
Basho's Travel Journal
Translated by Cid Corman
1-893996-31-X   5 x 7   128 pages $13.00

Volume 4
Heaven My Blanket, Earth My Pillow
Poems from Sung Dynasty China by Yang Wan-Li
Translated by Jonathan Chaves
1-893996-29-8   5 x 7   120 pages $14.00

Volume 3
10,000 Dawns
The Love Poems of Claire and Yvan Goll
Translated by Thomas Rain Crowe and Nan Watkins
1-893996-27-1   5 x 7   96 pages $13.00

Volume 2
There Is No Road
Proverbs by Antonio Machado
Translated by Mary G. Berg & Dennis Maloney
1-893996-66-2   5 x 7   120 pages $14.00

Volume 1
Wild Ways: Zen Poems of Ikkyu
Translated by John Stevens
1-893996-65-4   5 x 7   128 pages $14.00